A Greek Mosaic

A Greek Mosaic

Fay N. Kozas

 iUniverse®

A GREEK MOSAIC

iUniverse books may be ordered through booksellers or by contacting:

iUniverse
1663 Liberty Drive
Bloomington, IN 47403
www.iuniverse.com
1-800-Authors (1-800-288-4677)

ISBN: 978-0-5953-4540-3 (sc)
ISBN: 978-0-5957-9288-7 (e)

Print information available on the last page.

iUniverse rev. date: 08/29/2015

This book is dedicated to the American-born daughters
of all immigrants
and to the memory of my great-grandmother Anna whom I
never met but who is an inspiration to me

CONTENTS

Chapter One

Savoring Sweet Memories
of the Garment District*

I grew up in Manhattan's Garment District. My father died when I was nine days old. He and my mother had rented the railroad flat about ten months before I was born. My building was surrounded by big, tall, gloomy, forbidding-looking factories (some of them emitted filthy, polluted smoke from their smokestacks). Every day at about noon, the streets were filled with delivery men pushing racks of merchandise.

The various delicatessens and ethnic restaurants, their aromas wafting in the air, vied for the attention of the workers. A pungent odor of meat or garlic frying in oil or lard came from the Cuban restaurant (we called it Spanish) in my building. It had a back door that led to the hallway and from there to the street. Many times, customers took advantage of this layout, giving themselves a free meal.

Attached to my building was a Cuban cigar store, where cigars were rolled before being shipped all over the world. The Greek pastry shop around the corner filled the air with an aroma that was only topped by the delectable sweets it served, pastry on a par with nectar and ambrosia, the food of the gods. The honey-baked goods, the cinnamon and almond-topped cookies, the sugar cookies, the "tsoureki" or sweet bread, all transported even the most difficult-to-please customer to heaven on Earth.

1

Mary's Italian Bakery offered different kinds of breads—-white, whole wheat, semolina (with or without sesame seeds), rolls, and even Greek church bread. The Italian pastries would catch the eye of the passer-by and he would have difficulty deciding which bakery to choose.

The three Greek grocery stores, aside from advertising the "Miss Rhinegold Contest", were full of many kinds of olives, cheeses, grape leaves, herbs, and imported spices, all laid out in burlap sacks for the customer to view. Two groceries also had a butcher shop. There the Greeks could find the traditional Easter lamb, sheep heads known as "kefalaki", which are baked and served with lemon and oregano, sheep brains fried in oil, and tripe for soup and served with the sheep stomach in the dish. One shop was named Athens.

If you wanted ouzo, no need to worry. It was concocted in a house on Ninth Avenue and sold to a few trusted customers. It was stronger than the ouzo bottled in Greece. Ah, Bacchus, come and partake! For the god of wine and mirth, people would forget their vows. Under his influence, they would find escape from their trapped, unfulfilled married lives.

To a Greek, marriage vows are sacred. He stays married forever. Four stores in the neighborhood sold the "stefana" (wedding crowns), which are a must for any Greek wedding. They also carried "boubounieres" or favors. Made of porcelain or plastic and shaped like swans, pill boxes or turn-of-the century shoes, they're filled with Jordan almonds and given to each wedding guest.

I lived in a cold-water flat most of my childhood. The bathtub was in the kitchen and the bathroom was in the hallway. We boiled water just like the pioneers. The kerosene stove in the kitchen, whose smokestack went through the wall right up to the roof, served as our only means of heat. When I was nine, we were blessed with central heating, and our own private bathroom.

On hot, sultry, summer days, we went to the tarred roof to cool off. Up there I could see the clock tower lit up at night, and the Hotel Manhattan with its gigantic logo that kept changing colors. The "M" became pink, sky blue, then white.

Recently, after many years away, I went back to my old Garment District neighborhood. The Cuban restaurant is now Mexican. The cigar store is gone. So are the Greek pastry shop and the shoe-shine kiosk. The Greek travel agency is now a Starbucks. But the factory where my mother worked as a finisher before I was born is still there. My building's entrance had changed but the façade was the same. The super gave me a tour of the place that used to be my home. She showed me a renovated apartment renting for over a thousand dollars, an astronomical amount to me when I was a child.

I walked up the four flights of stairs. And there, to the right, was the door that once led to my three-room cold-water flat, to my childhood and to my past.

To a Greek, the birth of Christ symbolizes new beginnings full of hope. The Greek housewives start their baking early enough so that the two favorites-- "kourambiethes" (powdered sugar cookies) and "melomakarona" (honey-dipped walnut cookies) will adorn the Christmas table. As a child, I woke up to a table festooned with goodies. On the dresser in the living room stood our two-foot-tall, plastic Christmas tree with decorations the size of quarters. My mother had bought it for me when I was fifteen months old.

These days I rarely bake. Greek pastry shops take care of that for me. But on Christmas morning, I promise you, I wake up to the sight of a two-foot-tall plastic Christmas tree with decorations the size of quarters.

---

* Published in Newsday, "City Life", December 24th, 2003

Chapter Two

More New York Nostalgia

My parents were Greek immigrants. My father came to this country in 1924 but not through Ellis Island. He just came. He worked as a baker in a warehouse bakery on 42nd Street and 12th Avenue that supplied all the restaurants and hotels. Co-owned by a Greek and a Jew, it was named "Fotis and Fisher". My father joined the U.S. Army during World War Two and was stationed in New Jersey. He baked for the military and rose in the ranks to technical sergeant. When he was honorably discharged, he went to Cuba for his citizenship papers. At that time, Cuba and the U.S. were friendly. In the meantime, Fotis and Fisher closed down. My father embarked on the "Marine Carp", a passenger ship whose route included New York, Piraeus, Haifa, and Beirut.

My father married my mother in Greece and brought her to his furnished room on 28th Street and 8th Avenue. It had no stove, the bathroom was communal, the mattress was lumpy and the window looked out on a brick wall. The room was hardly big enough for one, let alone for two. Before my father got married, the landlady sub-rented it when he was away even though he always brought her the best cognac from Greece. On the day my father brought my mother there as a bride, the room was occupied.

My parents ate out. Eighth Avenue was full of Greek restaurants and Arabic night clubs such as the Britannia, the Port Said, and the Spartacus. The Spartacus served the best porgies. One day, my mother decided to make demi-tasse in the furnished room. She bought cotton, alcohol, matches, and an ibrik, a special little pot for the Turkish coffee the Greeks call Greek. She placed it on the alcohol-soaked cotton, lit the match, and could smell the aroma of the brewing coffee. So could the landlady. Storming into the room, she grabbed the ibrik from my mother's hand and threw it out.

Soon after, my parents moved to a fourth floor walk-up railroad flat in the Garment District that had neither heat nor hot water. My father's Jewish friends gave him their old clothes that were still brand new for his family in Piraeus. He disembarked loaded with gabardine coats and suits. Once, to avoid customs, he wore all the Fruit-of-the-Loom shirts they gave him and jumped into the Saronic Gulf after tying a rope around his waist and attaching it to a post on the ship. He swam to shore in the pouring rain and knocked on his sister's door in the middle of the night unloading his gifts like St. Nicholas. His name was Nick and a few years later, when I was nine days old, he died of coronary stenosis at forty-three.

That railroad flat was my first home. The day before Thanksgiving when I was nine years old, the smoke from our kerosene heating stove would not escape through the smokestack. Someone had thrown bricks down the opening on the roof. My mother consulted with the Greek owner of a grocery store. He knew many unemployed men who frequented the bar on our block. Would we mind if the worker were Black? Race was no object. The object was to get the job done.

He was available on Thanksgiving Day. However, we had been invited to spend the holiday with my godparents, as we did every year.

Early on Thanksgiving morning, there was a knock on our door. He rolled up his sleeves, unscrewed the smokestack, knelt on the linoleum floor, and removed the bricks. He went to the roof to continue. When he finished, my mother gave him a few dollars and asked him to sit at our table. We shared the chicken and the potatoes she had put in the oven and we had a nice conversation. Actually, he and I spoke English and I translated everything for my mom. At the dinner table, he told us that it was the best Thanksgiving he ever had.

Recently, I went to my old neighborhood. The building where my parents lived as newlyweds still stands. The night clubs are no longer. The Dixon Cafeteria, a haven for the Greeks who, over coffee, reminisced of their village "kafenio", is now a vanity store. That is where my godfather worked as a baker and every year I would go to remind him to bake my birthday cake. It was a sort of ritual. I always had the most beautiful, most delicious cake. When I was eleven years old, my godfather died of leukemia. The Pantheon, a Greek restaurant where my mother took me for dinner as a sign of her pride in me when I received my B.A. from Hunter College, is now a restaurant for the "meat and potatoes" kind of guy. The Cameo movie theater featured Russian movies during the week, switching to Greek on weekends. On some Friday afternoons, we went to see a free movie with our Greek school teacher. The name has changed. From the marquis I could tell that it now serves a certain "adult" clientele. The Barricini candy store has become part of the façade of the Port Authority.

The area is replete with stores selling fabrics, just as it was when I was growing up. My mother bought materials at three yards for a dollar and, being an excellent seamstress, fashioned them into clothes for me. Some fabrics, along with coffee beans and Lipton tea bags, were sent to my grandmother on the Greek island. The logos on the windows caught my eye-- "It's a material thing" or "The finest fabric that the world has to offer". In one window I saw 1930's Singer sewing machines on display. They are now collectors' items.

On 42nd Street I saw the Athenian gift shop, the McGraw Hill Building and the post office from which we sent my grandmother all those packages. The pharmacy on the corner of 9th Avenue where my mother bought powdered ammonia for a Greek cookie recipe is now a Commerce Bank. I saw the Poseidon Bakery and the Big Apple Meat Market. The hardware store that supplied us with wicks for our kerosene stove is no longer and neither is Mary's dress shoppe where my mother bought a yellow checked jacket with gold buttons, very much in style when I was a toddler. It was my mother's favorite and it still hangs in my closet.

I could see New Jersey on the horizon. Beyond it lies the home country. My father's ship is no longer in commission. Many things have changed but the one thing that has not changed is my love for my first neighborhood, the place I still call home.

Chapter Three

In the Beginning

I believe in old wives' tales. They are all true and very well-founded. According to a Greek one, God sent the Grim Reaper on a mission. He ordered him to bring Him the soul of a young man. When the Grim Reaper reached their threshold, his wife and two children were wailing bitterly. They pleaded with him and he felt sorry for them. He returned to his Maker empty-handed. God asked for an explanation. Upon hearing the explanation, God became very angry. He smacked the Grim Reaper across the face. The Grim Reaper lost his hearing.

He has been deaf to people's pleadings ever since.

Ever since the time of the Olympian gods, the Greeks have been fervent believers in dreams. At that time, they consulted the high priests to have them interpreted when they, themselves, could not. When the Greeks awaited a favorable wind before launching their ships for Troy, Agamemnon, King of Mycenae, dreamt of a flock of nine black birds flying high among the clouds, with a tenth at a distance. The high priest Kalhas was summoned to interpret this omen sent by Ypnos, the god of sleep. The priest informed them that their victory against the Trojans would take close to ten years to materialize and only after certain machinations, at that. Hence the creation of the Trojan horse and the rest is history.

Every child has a favorite fairy tale. Mine was Cinderella although, in retrospect, it should have been Rapunzel. Every little girl dreams of a prince--Prince Charming, who on his white horse and in his shining armor, will make her every dream come true. Sometimes, if it takes too long, it is King Charming who comes instead.

In child's play, charades took on an interesting form. I, with my neighbor's niece, threw our shoes down a flight of stairs in imitation of Cinderella's glass slipper that suffered the same fate in my book, in child's fantasy, in real life, at the ball, at the palace. Amazing! What a child's imagination can do! The little white octagonal marble floor tiles, set against the cream-colored stucco walls of the well-lit hallway, were all juxtaposed to the dull brown wooden banister that my neighbor's nephew held on to as he ran after my slipper. The prince put it on my foot. Aha! It fit! But alas, it was still leather. Like Rapunzel, I had a prince who frequented my tower. However, the prince could not rescue me.

In a fairy tale, the Princess has a mother who is a Queen and a father who is a King. In a fairy tale, the enemy cannot penetrate the tower. Rapunzel was safe behind hers. Mine, however, was not as invincible. My enemy, Death on horseback, struck at my tower until it came tumbling down like a stack of cards.

Ravaged by a high fever after giving birth to me, my mother had a dream while still in the hospital. She didn't need a high priest to interpret it. My father was pleading with a tall, dark, relentless black-clad stranger blocking his path. She woke up in a cold sweat and knew there would be no streets paved with gold in America for her. Without knowing about her dream, my father ordered the doctor to discharge us. Right then and there, the doctor complied. That night into the next morning, my father died. He died because his heart gave out and because the Grim Reaper makes no bargains.

Chapter Four

Child's Play

Perched on my little wooden stool on the fire escape four flights up....oops! I almost lost my balance. It's pretty wobbly up here, if you ask me. I must be careful lest I hurt myself. Boy, where did I learn this vocabulary word? "Lest"? I can't believe I said that because in real life, I don't know how to speak English. I only know how to speak Greek and even though I am four years old, I know how to recite the Greek alphabet because my mommy has taught me. I also know how to count from one to one-hundred in Greek and from one-hundred down to one. Boy, I can't believe my little brain can do all that! I love learning. When I grow up I'm going to be a teacher because I want to teach others what my mommy has taught me. I want to be a teacher so much! I play school with my dolls. They are my students. Sometimes they give me the right answer; sometimes they don't. When they don't, I get very upset.

Oops! There it goes again! Down, down, down. Four stories down. I can't seem to catch it. What is wrong with me? I must try harder. This one came so close yet it was out of reach. Out of reach....Everything for me is out of reach. I feel as if I am standing in front of a store window, looking at the display. I can't touch it; I can't have it. I can only stare at it.

"Fay, aren't you ashamed of yourself? What a waste!" My mother chastises me. She is angry. You see, everything with the Greeks has to do with honor and with shame. It is always, "Don't do anything to embarrass the family and the family name." So, I can't catch. What can I do? I'm no baseball super hero.

Yesterday, I was a poor catcher again. I'm so embarrassed. Sometimes I'm very good at catching; other times I'm not. Maybe it's his pitching. I don't know.

From my little throne I can see him with his brother and grandfather at their tenement window directly across from mine. Vast space and a bare, dreary cement yard separate us. He throws oranges and other fruit in my direction in an attempt to win my friendship. His Greek eyes are dark and sweet and his smile is warm and beautiful. I smile back. We understand each other. They are orphans, too.

One day, they all disappeared.

"I want to play with Terry."
"Don't bother them."
"I want to play with Terry."

Terry is my next-door neighbor's six-year-old granddaughter. She is rich, pretty, and very lucky. She has parents and a brother. They live in a private home in Queens and Terry gets anything she wants. When she goes through her wardrobe, she gives me her old clothes.

I am knocking on the door. My neighbor opens it, but my goodness, she looks angry.

"I want to play with Terry."

"Terry is busy."

Why did she slam the door in my face? Now I am standing here in the hallway in front of a closed door. My mother will be furious. You see, she doesn't like to bother anybody.

"Get in here. I told you to leave them alone."

My goodness. Nobody understands me. I am only four years old and I want to play. I am the only child in this entire building consisting of sixteen apartments. I am tired. Most of the time I play with my dolls and other toys because my mother can't take me to the park every day. My elderly widowed neighbor from downstairs has no children and loves me a lot. She reads to me very often. Mrs. Callas talks to me of strange places and of gods and goddesses. All these myths are fascinating. But I want to play....

Gee, how much time has gone by? I want to try again.

Knock, knock.

"What do you want?"
"I want to play with Terry."
"We are eating now. Terry can't play." BAM!!

Gee, what was that? Oh, she just slammed the door in my face. Oh, no! How do I tell my mother?

"Get in here!" I hear her screaming. "Get in here before I spank you." She is yanking me in and I am crying. If I had a father, I am thinking, if my father were alive, I would run to him to get away from you because he would love me so! Now I am bawling. I can't take this anymore. I want to play.

I knock again for the third time. I can't believe I'm so gutsy. I really, really want to play. This time, I didn't even get a chance to tell her what I want. She opened the door a crack and slammed it in my face.

Knock, knock.

"Who is it?"
"It is I."

Who is it, I'm asking myself? My next-door neighbor? What now?

My mommy makes her welcome. I know she is afraid of her. My mommy doesn't make anybody angry. I know why. There is no one to stand by her. I may be only four years old but I know a lot for my age. I observe. My mommy says she knows I'm smart because of the way I look around me. She says I know more than I let on.

"Helen doesn't want Terry to play with Fay." So Terry's mother is behind all this. Now she is looking at me. OH! OH! "Terry has a father and she has money. You don't. And when she grows up she will go to college and marry a doctor or a dentist."

I feel strange. I feel the walls closing in on me. I feel trapped in my tower with no escape. I want to cry but I am putting on a brave front. After all, I am only a child.

It is not a golden memory, but it ties me to my past.

Right after high school, she married a furrier's young aide.

Chapter Five

I Always Wanted a Doll House

I remember my mother on her knees scrubbing floors. She did housework to supplement her income. She dusted, swept, vacuumed, cleaned bathrooms, washed clothes and ironed. And yes, she did do windows.

I am tired of being dragged along on the subway at the crack of dawn. I want to sleep. I want to play like everyone else. I want to have a carefree, innocent childhood. But no, she drags me to all the houses she has to clean. What do I do all day? Nothing much. I sit on one of the chairs and I either look through my book or I play with a toy I have brought along. It gets boring for me.

I watch my mommy clean. I watch her get the pail, fill it with water and then pour something into it that takes my breath away. It takes her breath away, too. I know because of the face she makes as she is pouring. It bothers her so! Sometimes when she can't take it anymore, she faints. But nobody really cares. After all, she is only the cleaning lady.

I admire the houses. They are so big. They are all full of beautiful, elegant furniture. The children have their own bedrooms. I look at their toys from a distance but do not touch. My mommy has instructed me not to touch anything. She is afraid I will break something and they will not want her to work for them anymore. She really needs the $2.00 they will give her at the end of the day. Yes, $2.00 and that is better than nothing. Sometimes they give her lunch; sometimes they don't. If she eats, I eat.

The siblings get together with the neighborhood children. They want to play. Oh boy! I hope they invite me to play, too. I'm very careful with toys. I'm very careful with my toys, too. If I break any, my mommy doesn't have money to buy them for me again. The crowd enters the bedroom--the one that's full of toys. I noticed a doll house full of tiny furniture. The house was so big! It had so many rooms! These people are so rich even their dolls live in big houses. Maria's bed has such a beautiful bedspread. It's all white and pink. It's got ruffles on the sides. Her curtains match her bedspread. She has such a nice room! I have been in her bedroom once or twice before. But not to play. Maria wanted to style my hair. You see, I have these beautiful, long braids and Maria wants to turn them into banana curls. She takes out some white, narrow material and wraps it around clumps of my hair. She leaves it on like that for hours. When my mommy is ready to leave, Maria removes the wrapping and, presto! My braids have become beautiful banana curls! She doesn't do this too often. Only when she is in a good mood and when I haven't expressed an interest to play with anybody. Maybe she will do that again today.

Strange! They are throwing glances at me but they seem so angry. What did I do? I don't remember doing anything I wasn't supposed to. They all go into Maria's bedroom and shut the door. I get up from my seat and approach. I knock on the door but they do not respond. I hear them giggling. I knock again. I don't hear a thing. I want to play. I knock again and call out her name. Her brother opens the door a crack, looks at me, and says sternly, "Go away." He slams the door shut. Why should they let me in? After all, I am only the cleaning lady's daughter.

Chapter Six

Circles

Greek, Greek, and more Greek. Every Greek child is taught to speak it, to write it, to read it, to accept it, to revere it. You think Greek, you speak Greek, you act Greek, you eat Greek, you drink Greek, you dance Greek, you dream Greek. Even your nightmares are Greek.

One of my favorite excursions was a trip to Central Park, an oasis in the middle of the asphalt jungle, a torrential downpour on cracked, scorched land. All those shades of green, as far as the eye could see, coming together to form one mosaic--a mosaic of nature at its best. Acres and acres of grass, trees, leaves, bushes. When I looked up I didn't see a full sky; I saw pieces of it through the intertwining branches that were laden with leaves and more leaves. The squirrels scrambled up the trees for some acorns, they scrambled back down and ran across the grass, the birds flew across the sky, and the ducks swam around on the pond. To me, the ducks were the most vulnerable of all, a pebble's throw from the curious onlookers. Horse-drawn carriages, carriages like Cinderella's took the tourists around the park for the right price. And there were picnics on the grass. Picnics and music.

The music was strange yet it resembled Greek music. The sad, mellow, whining, melodic tunes with the high notes, the low notes, picking up the tempo, allegro, a sad blare, a drawn out high note, nostalgic, sentimental. The dancers were going around in a circle but that was not strange to me. Greeks also dance in a circle--they even go around in circles and even their speech is roundabout as they can never get to the point. These dancers danced from right to left. Right to left? What? When Greeks dance, they go from left to right--just the way we read--from left to right. But this was klezmer. What? Klezmer? The music of the Jewish soul. Starry-eyed, I was taking it all in. Before I knew it, an elderly gentleman approached me and gently pulled me into their circle. What was I doing? Was this right? I was fascinated. I didn't even have trouble following along; it all came so naturally to me. I was dancing up a storm.

Dancing is in my blood. I was born dancing. I was dancing in the delivery room. When I hear that bouzouki music, I am rejuvenated. The bouzouki is the national instrument of Greece. It has a soul, a heart, a voice. Only a handful of Greek men have the gift and the knowledge to play it. It is sacred.

> The bouzouki is
> national organ of Greece
> and it is sacred
>
> When a Greek dances,
> he dances from left to right,
> just the way he reads.
>
> The Greeks throw money
> on the floor and they break plates.
> Greeks know how to live.
>
> Zorba was a Greek.
> He knew the meaning of life
> and why we are here.
>
> The Greek band plays on
> fulfilling all the requests,
> and the dancers dance.
>
> One of the dances,
> by the name of the "syrto",
> speaks to a Greek's heart.
>
> The syrto, you see,
> is the dance of the islands
> imitates the sea

forward and back steps
as the sea's waves ebb and flow
the waves ebb and flow

The dancer in front
holds a plain white handkerchief
representing foam

Sometimes I attend
Jewish cultural affairs
to be entertained.

At klezmer concerts
dancers go from right to left,
just the way they read.

I think of the Greeks
as they dance from left to right
keeping to the beat.

What is confusion?
Confusion is when you go
around in circles.

So now, picture this:
The Greeks dancing with the Jews
concentric circles

as the band plays on,
left, right, left, right, left
all around they go

left, right, left, right, left
I am left here wondering
which of them is right.

Forbidden fruit was beginning to look good.

Chapter Seven

A Black Tie Affair

So, if he has to be Greek, he has to be Greek. Greek girls are brought up, brainwashed actually, to marry a nice Greek boy. A Jew, you say? What's a Jew? He has to be Greek. We have to know the family. The prince would come and call to Rapunzel to let down her hair. He would climb up to the tower, a priest would be kept in the closet (kept there for such purposes), they would get married, and live happily ever after. Right? Wrong! Nobody said it would be easy. A Greek prince does not climb up to the tower all too easily. He remembers his mother's stern warning: "Don't do anything with a Greek girl, I'll kill you." Dream on, Rapunzel.

Greeks dream, too. They always dream. If it is not about marrying a rich American girl and getting a green card, it is about marrying a rich American girl and getting a green card. Either way, they win. A Greek must always win. You see, a Greek's ego is very delicate. Like fruit, it should not be bruised.

Speaking of fruits--
Right after I got back from my first trip to Greece, I armed myself with bravado and invited a Greek member of the opposite sex to a very formal affair in an endeavor to win his heart. I am not certain which is easier--winning somebody's heart or somebody's mind? Oh, did I say mind? Oh, well....

"What if he rejects the offer?" Mother Superior asked. "Since when do nice Greek girls take the initiative?" She didn't want a loose daughter.

Remembering my Jewish friend and college classmate Linda, I replied, "He won't say no." Linda had been taught very well by her parents. She had high self-esteem.

Guess what? He didn't say no, but then I didn't know what I now know. He didn't know what a black tie affair was.

"Oh, I have a black tie I can wear." Huh?!! He would wear a black tie that he happened to have hanging in the closet next to his red tie, blue tie, green tie and every other tie on the rack. I was fit to be tied!

At the Plaza Hotel? The Plaza? Where's that? My mother is an immigrant. She knows the Plaza Hotel. She's had coffee at the Plaza. She has been wined and dined at the Plaza.

I had let down my hair but there was no way this Romeo would climb up to my tower. Quickly, I pulled up my locks. And locked my lattices. I thought of an excuse to give him a few days later and blamed it all on my mother and her ill health. I will never know what the Penguin Ball was like. Not that I lose any sleep over it. I'm just grateful I was able to disentangle myself from this mess and break all ties.

Chapter Eight

Crossing Paths

Boy, I'm so excited! Today I'm graduating from Junior High School. Thank goodness it's not raining because my white dress and shoes would be ruined. I'm not too happy with this dress; it's not really me. The full skirt accentuates my already big hips and the spaghetti straps are just too much for me to handle. I'm not used to this. Then it's got this vest with the long see-through sleeves. I just know that as the day goes on, it will be so hot, I will absolutely die in this vest. I could take it off; no, I can't. I'm embarrassed. I don't want to go around with this spaghetti-strap top. Why did I buy this dress in the first place? But the other dress I thought I liked was even worse. That didn't even have a vest. I picked it after I returned this one but then I brought it back to the store to exchange it for this one again, the dress I am wearing. What confusion! The saleslady was having a fit. I really drove her out of her mind, and only because I couldn't make up my mind. Oh, well, it's done now. I just have to suffer. As soon as I step outside, the whole world will know I'm graduating. I will stick out like a sore thumb. Thank goodness it's early morning and the factory delivery boys and the workers have not begun to circulate yet. I don't want any of them whistling at me. But why would they whistle? I feel so unattractive. Some of them whistle at anybody. How does my hair look? It's too short and curly. I just wish it were long and flowing. But it's not.

I can't believe this day has finally arrived. Although I somewhat enjoyed my years in junior high school, it is time to move on. I want to meet new people and make new friends. Sometimes it wasn't easy being with these classmates. We had the same subjects and moved around together from class to class and, except for gym and shop and possibly foreign language, we were together all day, every day. You see, I was the new kid on the block entering seventh grade. Most of my classmates knew each other from elementary school. It was so hard for me to blend in. Sometimes I felt like a square peg trying to fit into a round hole. They made me cry a lot. They gave me to understand I didn't belong. In a few days it will be all over. Each of us will go to high school; maybe not to the same high school. That's even better for me. I don't want to run into them. I want to get away from them, as far away as I possibly can.

Oh, oh! Who is this man approaching me with a smile on his face?

"I know it's a big day for you and I want to wish you the best."

"Thank you."

Off he goes. From his accent I can tell he is a Jew. He breaks my heart. A stranger....

His daughter, if he has one, is a very lucky girl.

How many more stops to 59th Street? Who is this woman sitting in front of me? She looks awfully familiar. Let me hold on to the hand strap before I lose my balance and fall. I'm afraid of serious injuries and hospitals. We don't even have health insurance if it ever came to that. The thought scares the daylights out of me. If we ever need hospitalization, who will pay for it? Where will we end up? They will probably take us to some horrendous hospital and throw us in some windowless room and not pay any attention to us at all. What will I do if anything happens to my mother—if she gets suddenly sick or if she gets hit by a car or truck? I will go absolutely crazy. What will she do if I get sick or if I get hit by a car? What will she do if I die? After all, I am her pride and joy. What am I doing? Why am I thinking like this? I can't wait to go home and get into my cocoon and just shut everything and everybody out. I feel so safe at home. But I have a long day ahead of me. Oh, well, too bad I didn't get a seat. This woman in front of me looks awfully familiar and if she is who I think she is, she has not recognized me. I should speak up. What have I got to lose?

"Excuse me, are you Helen?"

Startled, she looks at me and shakes her head yes. How long has it been? The door....bam!.... I want to play....bam!....Forbidden.... Not good enough....A doctor....A dentist....fur....

"I don't think you remember me. I'm Fay. Your mother was our next-door neighbor on the West Side."

"Oh, Fay, of course I remember you. How are you?" Does she really care? I wonder. If I could only read her mind. But what does it matter? She seems surprised and pleased. It seems as if she has mellowed and has become condescending. She fills me in. Terry has a baby girl. What is she saying? It's hard to hear above the din. It's not important. She fills me in regarding everybody else. I feel uncomfortable. I can't breathe. I feel ashamed. I feel poor.

"I'm going to Hunter College. I have classes. I want to be a teacher," I hear myself saying. "We live in Astoria now." I keep babbling on and on. I don't know what else to say.

The train is pulling into the station. The doors are opening and I must get off. I say good-bye. The train pulls out of the station. I head for Hunter College and my dreams.

What a coincidence! Was it a coincidence?

Nothing is ever a coincidence.

Chapter Nine

Special Delivery

Dear Mommy,

I am writing this letter to you as I'm sitting in front of my computer--oh, did I tell you? I bought a computer. I travel through it, because of it, with it, to all parts of the world. I go to our beloved Symi. Symi. If you were sitting here with me, you would see the island of your birth, the island where you grew up, the island of our ancestors. You would even hear Greek music while watching the pictures of Symi on the web site.

I often think of our first trip to Symi--actually, my first trip to Symi. You had been away from the island for a total of fifty-three years. Remember what you said to me when we got there? Although it has been sixteen years since our trip, I remember everything. Those were beautiful, happy days and I have golden memories of them. You told me that even though it was the island of your birth, you didn't belong. You were a stranger. You said you felt like a stranger in America and like a stranger in Symi. You said you left the island when you were a young woman and returned with white hair and a hump on one side of your back. Mommy, that hump served as an indication and a reminder of the hard life you had in America. But you didn't have one wrinkle on your face. You had such soft, smooth skin. That's because you never plopped any make-up on your face when you were a young woman. Mommy, you were so beautiful! I asked you how you could have stayed on that island being that I felt so constricted. The sun on the horizon seemed so close. I could reach out and almost touch it with my hand as it danced on the Aegean. The sea itself seemed so narrow. And the island seemed so small. You told me you stayed because you hadn't known anything better. You had to leave in search of a better life.

One wintry day in March of 1935, you boarded the ship headed for Piraeus. Your widowed mother dressed in black, a black kerchief covering her braids, her braids that you so admired, those braids wrapped around her head, walked you, her eldest daughter, to the harbor. With you, went all the neighbors, relatives, and friends. You bade everyone good-bye and held your elderly mother in your arms. On the ship's deck, you waved good-bye. The ship bellowed, emitted smoke, and pulled out of the harbor. All the figures on the shore became smaller and smaller until they resembled pencil dots. When the ship made a turn around the dock where the clock tower is situated by the post office, still chiming every hour on the hour to this day, they disappeared altogether. How melodic that chime was to your ears! Your mother remained standing on the dock for a long time. She prayed for you. She prayed that you should have a good trip. She prayed that you should get to your destination safe and sound. She prayed that you should have a good future. After all, you were her first-born and you were her pride and joy. You were special. She was sending Piraeus a special delivery. I know you carried this image in your heart all your life. You never spoke of it and about how you felt. This image I carry in my imagination all my life. It is very painful. I don't know how you did it. The pain of separation is indescribable. The pain of separation is unbearable. I wouldn't wish it on my enemy. You never saw your mother again. But at the time, you didn't know it.

We had a great time in Greece. We only stayed in Symi for five days but I got to know the island of our roots. I met your childhood friends. You told me many things. We were mother and daughter. We bonded. I was ecstatic. You told me that I was your sunshine, your happiness, your life. You told me you were so happy when you were expecting me. When the doctor told you that you were pregnant, you were jubilant being you were on in years. But things happen. You wouldn't have it any other way. And here I am. You told me the delivery was difficult. You were too weak and frail. Then the doctor told you that you had given birth to a "very nice baby". Those were his words, you said. Your very own baby. You made me feel so good because I was so wanted. I was your special delivery. You told me what you felt when the doctor let you hold me for the first time. You were afraid that someone would switch me in the hospital and you would lose me to another mother. My father laughed and said things like that don't happen in America. You always remembered my hair. I was born with black hair. The black hair that I wore in banana curls and then in braids until I was five years old. I was just like my "yiayia". You told me my little head was so round--just like a ball. Oh, by the way, my hair isn't black anymore. It is frosted. I changed my image. I don't think you would recognize me. But I think you would like it. I'm not the same without you anymore, Mommy. I miss you.

I am not living in our old apartment. You know which one I'm talking about. It was never the same after that. So I did something you always wanted me to do. I bought my own place. I bought a condominium. It's really very nice, roomy, and beautiful. I like it a lot. Your favorite armchair is in my living room. But it is empty. I look at it when I walk in and hope to see you sitting there, but you're not. As I'm coming up the path I raise my eyes in hopes of seeing you by the window, expecting me. I don't see your visage anymore.

I remember our previous apartment. It was a duplex. We had an eat-in kitchen and an L-shaped living room/dining room. We used to knead bread and roll cookies on the kitchen table. Remember? We used to argue because you would get me so mad. You wanted the Greek cookies I shaped to be just so and I would get annoyed. I don't have that table anymore. I gave it away, along with three of the chairs, because in my new place, there is no room. I kept one chair to remind me of you and of the times we sat at that table and had breakfast, lunch, and dinner together. I didn't want to part with it. Now in my new place I eat my breakfast standing up in my kitchen. Do you remember our dining room set? The china closet with the concave/convex glass door? It stood on carved wooden feet shaped like a lion's paw. That was a special piece. I think it was called "turn-of-the-century". Do you remember the old-fashioned heavy wooden table with the balloon legs? What about the four chairs that wore the covers you made? We had dinner on that table on holidays and on our special occasions. There was a sideboard that went with it. That was a rare piece, too. I could never force myself to like that entire ensemble but we kept it. We kept it because....well, we got used to it. We got used to it and it became a part of us. It wouldn't fit in my new home so I sold it to a dealer. But before I did, I took pictures of the whole room. I took pictures of the whole room so that I should remember.

I walk in to an empty place. I try to keep busy so that I should forget. But I always remember. Sometimes I live in the past. If I could turn back the clock, I would. But what good would that do? I would have to relive the pain of losing you once again. When you got very sick, I was devastated. I couldn't believe that was happening to you. I know you were old, but to me you were my Mommy. I never saw you as an old woman. I never saw you as a human.

To me, you were my Mommy and that made you special and superhuman. When I lost you, I got very sick. I didn't want to go home. I walked the streets at midnight in the dead of winter. I slept until the afternoon and into the early evening. I didn't want to get up. Many times, I didn't go to work. I wanted desperately to turn back the clock. I wanted to tell you one more time that I loved you. I wanted to hug you and squeeze you tightly in my arms. But most of all, I wanted to do a lot of things I hadn't done when you were here.

I want you to come to my new place to see it. I want you to sit at my new dining room set and have coffee and cookies. I promise, I will make them just the way you like. Sit with me and talk to me. Tell me the stories you used to tell me when I was a child. When I was your special child. Let us be friends again. Let us bond one more time. Sit in your armchair, Mommy. Let me see you sitting in it when I walk in. Stand by the window and look to see if I'm coming up the path. Make me feel loved and wanted. I promise, I will be good. You always told me that I was the best daughter in the whole wide world. I used to tell you that you were the best mother in the whole wide world. Despite our differences and disagreements.

I wrote you this letter as I'm sitting here in front of my computer. I'm about to come to a close now. I wrote this letter just for you. Especially for you. I want to send it to you. I want to send you my letter so that you should read it. But where can I send it? I have no forwarding address. I feel so lost. Tell me what to do the way you used to tell me when you were here. It is almost four years. Four long years. I can't believe that so much time has gone by. I don't know where it all went. Sometimes, I throw myself into my work to lose all track of time. When I remember, I feel so lost. I hardly ever felt lost when you were here. Where should I send my letter? This is a special letter. This is a special letter for a special mother. How should I send it? Should I send it return receipt requested? Or should I send it by registered mail? Mommy, when it comes to you, I want to send this letter only one way--by special delivery.

Love and kisses,
To Feaki Sou
Your Fay

P.S. Mama, s'agapo.

Chapter Ten

A Navigation

This is about a voyage--a navigation.

In our culture a sailor is respected.

Rigging a vessel

She took the little one

and set out

on a voyage

fighting the waves incessantly

inundated

tremendous tumultuous tsunamis

out of breath

out of hope

They searched the forbidding horizon

frantically

She and the child were

tossed and pushed

tossed and pushed

toward the Unknown

Grabbing the helm

She steered the ship

into a cove

The anchor gripped the sand

and held

because my Mother was a Captain

sailing on the Sea of Life

The Greek version of A Navigation

ΕΝΑ ΤΑΞΙΔΙ

Αρμάτωσαν εις την ζωή κι'οι δυό ένα βαπόρι
Και θαλασσοπαλέψανε η Μάνα με την κόρη.

Δεν είχανε ούτε καιρό γύρω τους να κυττάξουν
Γιατί γύρευαν πως και πως λιμάνι για ν'αράξουν.

Συχνά αναρωτιώντουσαν: «Τι άραγε να γίνη;»
Μα ήταν Καπετάνισσα στην πλώρη η Ειρήνη.

Εκείνη ενθαρρύνθηκε και πήρε το τιμόνι
Και άρχισε σιγά–σιγά γαλήνη να απλώνη.

Και έτσι επεράσανε τα μαύρα χρόνια εκείνα
Γιατί ήταν η Μάνα μου δεύτερη Μπουμπουλίνα.

Chapter Eleven

The Sea and the Greeks

For some cultures, sponge diving is not only a way of life, it is life. Classified as many-celled animals, the sponges multiply by fertilizing eggs as the sperm passes through a cleavage. Each contains many pores or passages lined by cells. It is said that the sponges of the Mediterranean, being extremely soft, are the best kind. The sponges of the Red Sea are second best; those of the West Indies, being coarse and less durable, are the poorest in quality. Each sponge is made of a unique framework and is as individual as a snowflake or a person's fingerprints.

At the turn of the twentieth century, the sponge industry was thriving in Symi and Kalymnos, two Dodecanese islands. Most of the thirty thousand inhabitants in Symi were associated with the sea. If the Greeks are islanders, the sea is in their blood. It is a given. The sea flows in their veins and sustains them. It makes their hearts beat. It is their blood, their oxygen, their life. The sponge divers sailed with their vessels every April, leaving their families behind, and returned every October. Their loved ones prayed for their safe return and made offerings to the Virgin Mary and to various saints. Women were left widows and children were left orphans when the pitiless sea claimed lives. Sometimes, the divers were brought back on stretchers because the sea broke their spirits and destroyed their bodies but did not take their souls.

Before diving into the forbidding waters, the diver made the sign of the cross three times. Heavy garb protected him from the sub-zero temperatures of the sea while oxygen flowed through a tube attached to his helmet. He would not dive a second time in one day for fear of getting the bends and remaining a cripple. His life was in God's hands; in God's hands and in the hands of the "kolaoutze'ri" who tugged at his tube as he stood on deck to let the diver know that he only had two minutes before he should start ascending. The kolaoutze'ri, therefore, had to be a brother or trusted friend. Timing meant life or death. The divers who ignored the warning ended up on a bed of pain until their dying day. The Symean divers, it was said, did not wear an outfit and some could hold their breath for many minutes at a time. If we rely on the vivid imagination of the Greeks, the youths were able to hold their breath for even half an hour or more! When the sponges were brought to the island, they were laid out to dry before being pruned or trimmed. The rough edges were cut with a special pair of scissors, allowing the sponges to breathe. Then they were sold, as their purpose was multi-fold.

My maternal great grandmother Anna had seven children to feed. Widowed at an early age, she had to become resourceful to keep her family from starving. She baked bread. But bread becomes moldy. How many days does it keep without refrigeration as that was unheard of on the island in the late 1800's? She baked bread and re-baked it the next day, selling it as toast. She did business with the captains of the sponge vessels. She baked; they bought. She made a lot of money. She raised five daughters and two sons. The sea was good to her.

One of her daughters was my grandmother. She was happily married and it didn't matter to my grandfather that she was seven years his senior. He worshipped her.

My grandfather was a boatswain on a sponge vessel. He studied the stars and predicted the weather. The crew members depended on him. His wife and two daughters on the island depended on him as well.

Greek sailors say the sea is very cruel. They describe it by giving it female traits--cunning, unpredictable, unfaithful, volatile, conniving, charming as a kitten, fickle. However, it is her heartlessness that makes the sea so desirable to sailors. She penetrates their veins, their souls, their inner beings. Like a magnet, she pulls them to her; like a geyser, she spits them out and leaves them on the shore to die. I am reminded of the alluring Sirens in Greek mythology. The magnetized sailors followed the mellifluous voices only to be devoured, their bones thrown on the sand to rot in the hot, unbearable sun. Odysseus, King of Ithaca, saved his men from this danger on their way back from Troy by filling their ears with wax. Instructing his sailors to tie him to the mast, they were not to untie him no matter how hard he should try to free himself. Odysseus was the only one to hear the arias of Sygia, Lefkosia, and Parthenope and live to talk about it.

Like the Sirens, the sea beckons the sailors. Her pull is so strong that she has the power to drive the men insane. Because of her, they hallucinate. They see islands and ships on the horizon--ships that have sunk and have been resting on the ocean floor for hundreds of years. These ships send signals. Their captains send an SOS. They ask for help. The men hear voices. The voices cry out. The savior ships head for the horizon to offer assistance. The horizon broadens and becomes more distant. The ships pursue the endangered vessel. The latter becomes elusive and more distant, yet it continues to signal for help. The sailors refuse to give up. If the cards were reversed, they would want the nearest ship to do the same. They see a pair of beautiful, exotic green eyes staring at them. They belong to a woman. The blonde, wavy hair flows down her back while her hands grasp the side of the ship. She looks at the men, tears streaming down her face, and asks: <ΖΕΙ Ο ΜΕΓΑΣ ΑΛΕΞΑΝΔΡΟΣ;> Is Alexander the Great living? All the Greek sailors know the answer to that question. They remember the plight of the general who conquered areas of the Western world and the Far East and whose corpse was decapitated by the furious and jealous Persian King Darius. Alexander's sister, unable to cope with her loss, cried uncontrollably. The Greek gods, taking pity on her when they saw her drowning in her own tears, gave her the body parts required to survive in a watery element. She grabs the ship's railing with her hands and swings her tail to and fro. She has the strength to sink the ship. The sailors look at her with compassion, and tell her exactly what she wants to hear: <ΖΕΙ ΚΑΙ ΒΑΣΙΛΕΥΕΙ ΚΑΙ ΤΟΝ ΚΟΣΜΟ ΚΥΡΙΕΥΕΙ..> He is alive and well and is conquering the world. She lets go the ship. Content, she swims to her part of the world to await the next vessel. Suddenly, the sailors notice something in their midst that was not there before. It is a black cat. It looks at the men with her mysterious eyes, purrs, and cuddles up to them. How she got on the ship is a mystery. No one has carried her on board.

The sea makes the men forget. Like Odysseus's men who ate of the lotus flower and forgot their past, so the sailors forget their homelands, their wives, their families. In a stupor, they only cling to the sea and remember nothing else. They are enticed by her, they fall in love with her, they marry her. The sea becomes their wife. She is a woman. Like a woman, she charms. Like a woman, she forgets. Like a woman, she is unfaithful. Like a woman, she kills. No one can predict her moods and no one can trust her. But she commands respect.

My mother has golden memories of her father. He idolized his two daughters. He sailed to exotic places and came back to the island six months later with the boat full of sponges gathered from the ocean floor off the coast of North Africa. His gifts, such as azure, velour slippers from Tripoli for his two daughters and little grandniece, were equally exotic. Gold stars strewn across the top of each slipper were in opposition to the stars he studied strewn across a cold, dark sky.

At the beginning of the twentieth century, in the year one thousand nine hundred and one, the sponge vessel his brother worked on was chosen by destiny to make history. Its fate was tied to something that had occurred over one thousand years before. The "Efterpe" was sailing in the Mediterranean where the sponges were plentiful, bringing tremendous profits. One of the divers dove, cut the sponges off the reef, and shoved them into his duffel bag. Lo and behold! Something caught his attention, beckoning him. Was he hallucinating? Maybe; maybe not. An arm signaled him to approach. He was mesmerized. Disregarding the kolaoutze'ri, he swam toward it. Behind boulders covered with beautiful, colorful starfish and shells, was a marble statue of a youth, arm extended, body flexed. Tired of standing, he had shifted his weight while waiting to be rescued.

It was brought to the surface by a special oceanic crew skilled in such missions. After being studied and analyzed, it was categorized as a classical statue, probably stolen while in transport to or from Rome many years before. The sculptor of "The Youth of Antikythera" as the statue was named, was no other than Alkamenis, a student of Phidias during the Golden Age of Greece. A contemporary of Pericles, Phidias oversaw the construction of the Parthenon and supervised Kallicrates and Iktinos, its architects. His marble statue of Zeus, adorned with ivory and gold, was considered one of the seven wonders of the ancient world. Sitting on his throne, the father of all gods held the thunderbolt and the lightning. Unfortunately, the statue is no longer. The gold was melted down and made into weapons used during the Peloponnesian Wars, c.430 B.C.– 405 B.C. The Greek gods are no longer. They disappeared with the progress of time and with the onset of Christianity.

The crew members on the Efterpe were stunned at the find and took it as an omen. Their vessel had been singled out. Efterpe. That was the name of their ship. But Efterpe was no ordinary name. She was one of the nine Muses. Her father was Zeus and her mother Mnemosyne--a name that in Greek means "to be remembered and never forgotten". Each Muse represented either the arts or the universe. It is through the endowment and sustenance of the arts that a culture remains alive throughout eternity. Kleo, the Muse of history, praised the evolution of city-states and dominions. Thalia, the Muse of comedy, thrived when the ancient Greeks performed hilarious theatrical productions, especially those of Aristophanes. In contrast, Melpomene sang of Greek tragedies. Thus, Sophocles, Euripides, and Aeschylus had won her favor. She was always pictured holding a mask. Terpsichore was in her glory at dance performances and always held a stringed instrument such as a lyre. Erato, whose name is rooted in the word "eros", sang of love. Polymnia leaned against a mountain and sang religious and historic hymns. Kalliope, holding a blank slate and a writing utensil, sang of heroic deeds such as those immortalized by Homer in his epic, **The Iliad**. Ourania was the Muse of the heavens and held a globe and a compass. Then there was Efterpe. Efterpe was the Muse of lyric poetry.

Everything that was happening was surreal. It was flowing rhythmically like the waves of the sea that ebb and flow, ebb and flow. It was flowing rhythmically like the words in a line, in a stanza, in a poem, in lyric poetry. Everything happening around the Efterpe was mythical. Yet it was real.

It is over one thousand years since the Roman vessel sailed the Mediterranean. Three-hundred-sixty-five-thousand days. And more. People still talk about it.

One April night before my grandfather sailed for the barbarian coasts, he hammered a gold coin on the threshold of their home. He told my grandmother to keep it there for good luck until he returned.

Word reached my grandmother that my grandfather's sponge vessel had been sunk by a submarine off the coast of North Africa. First she cried. Then she pulled her hair and screamed out in pain. Then came the disbelief and the denial. She almost lost her mind. Madly in love with him, she waited for him until the day she died. She always thought that he would open the door and walk in. But he never did.

Chapter Twelve

Sacred Soil

With a palette,

I would like to paint a picture

of Symi in my heart.

My grandmother, with love,

planted a grapevine arbor in her courtyard.

It took root in the Earth

and was embraced by the soil.

Thus nurtured, it blossomed

and its branches grew

and were transplanted

in my heart.

I extend my arms and embrace you

oh, my Past, Present, and Future.

I embrace you and I hold you tightly

in my arms

glorious island of my Ancestors

in my arms in my heart

the grapevine

mirrored in my grandmother's smile

on Symi's sacred soil.

ΧΩΜΑ ΙΕΡΟ

Αγαπημένη Σύμη μου
πατρίδα του Νιρέα,
στην αγκαλιά σου επέρασα
πάρα πολύ ωραία.
Μ'ένα πινέλο
στην καρδιά θέλω να ζωγραφίσω
μία εικόνα της Σύμης μου.
Το άγιο το χώμα της θέλω να προσκυνήσω.
Το άγιο το χώμα της θέλω να το φιλήσω.
Με δένει με το παρελθόν
και με γυρίζει πίσω.
Κληματαριά εις την αυλή
φύτεψε η γιαγιά μου.
Οι ρίζες μπλέχτηκαν στη γη
το χώμα την αγκάλιασε
ποτίστηκε και άνθισε
και έφτασαν οι κλώνοι της
και μπήκαν στην καρδιά μου.
Σύμη μου, χώμα ιερό, χώμα αγαπημένο
το μέλλον μου και παρελθόν
για πάντα και προς το παρόν
ανοίγω τις αγκάλες μου
και σε κρατώ κλεισμένο
μέσα στην αγκαλιά μου
νησάκι, Σύμη μου, μικρό
νησάκι δοξασμένο
σφιχτά μέσα εις την καρδιά
μαζί με την κληματαριά
που φύτεψε εις την αυλή
χρόνια πριν η γιαγιά μου.
Αγαπημένη Σύμη μου
πατρίδα των προγόνων μου
θα σ'αγαπώ όσπου να ζω
και θέλω να'ρθω να σε δω
λίγες φορές ακόμα.
Οι ρίζες μου, το Είναι μου
οι ρίζες της κληματαριάς
το χαμόγελο της γιαγιάς
ευρίσκονται, Ω Σύμη μου,
στο ιερό σου χώμα.
Γεια σου, Σύμη!

Chapter Thirteen

Sacrifices

What is a sacrifice? That depends. For some people it means one thing; for others it means something else. If you give up your lunch period to tutor one of your students, it is a sacrifice. If you give up your seat to an elderly person on the subway, it is a sacrifice. If you give your sandwich to the hungry, it is a sacrifice. In ancient Greece, right before the Greek ships sailed for Troy, Agamemnon, King of Mycenae, sacrificed his daughter Iphigeneia at the altar in exchange for a favorable wind. Now, that was a sacrifice. If you have to relocate because of demographics forced on you by the government, you sacrifice. If your land is invaded by an enemy country, will you sacrifice? What is a sacrifice? Judge for yourself.

Picture this: Hugging and kissing your daughter good-bye as she boards the ship for other ports, wondering when and if you will see her again, hugging and kissing your widowed mother good-bye as you board the ship for Piraeus, wondering when and if you will see her again.... bidding your childhood home good-bye, the grapevine, the church in which you were baptized, the alley where you played as a child, the picturesque alleys of the island, your friends, your classmates, your playmates....

For nineteen hours and more, the ship sailed on, stopping every so often in between at various islands to discharge passengers and to take on additional ones. Getting off for a very brief stay on the island of Rhodes, my mother continued on her way to Piraeus with her suitcase full of clothes and her soul full of dreams. Symi became an image embedded in her mind, etched in her heart, and brought with her to the New World as a bride with my father many years later, after World War Two. If I could turn back the clock....if only I could change some things....What human has such powers?

Picture this: war-torn Piraeus, the largest harbor in all of Greece....war-torn Athens, the capital city of Greece....famine, lice, fear, despair

The dead were strewn on the streets of Athens. An emaciated dead woman lay on the sidewalk with an infant suckling her breast. Horrified and moved by the sight, the two women walking by plucked the infant from its mother's breast and took it home. They gave it food and shelter. The child never knew its mother. He was not told of this event. For everything there is a price. The scene was immortalized in bronze by a sculptor from the island of Symi. Named "The Mother of the War", the statue is on display in a museum in Paris.

The sirens began to blare right before the bombs fell. People were used to these attacks and went to bed dressed, ready to run. They pushed and shoved inconsiderately on their way to the trenches because it was every man for himself. Life didn't matter as long as it was not his life. What mattered was survival. My mother ran to the trenches to escape and to survive. No one considered the filth, the contamination, the stench, the spread of disease, or the lice. One night, my mother assumed there would be no attack. At the sound of the sirens, she ran out of the house, with her family, in her nightgown and slippers. At the end of the raid, she realized that she had lost one of her slippers. Devastated, she looked for it because she had fashioned it with her own hands and her creativity. However, it was useless. On the ground in front of her, was another's shoe. Having no choice, my mother put it on. Some people had lost lives and limbs. A slipper was nothing.

One night, a ship docked in the harbor in Piraeus was bombed. It exploded upon impact. A humongous metal piece, weighing hundreds of pounds, flew all the way across the city. It went through a roof and killed the couple sleeping in their bedroom. It barely missed the home of those who, years later, would become my mother's in-laws.

My mother spent the war years in Piraeus being miserable and poor. It was all one and the same--a non-ending nightmare. She told me horror stories that would make one's hair stand on end. Such was the cruelty of the enemy. They were merciless. Their acts reeked of the macabre, the inhumane, the surreal. But they were real. It is many years later as I am writing this. The acts of the enemy, whoever he may be depending on one's perspective, are still the same. They haven't changed. It seems as if all the enemies have gone to the same school and have taken the same courses: Torture 101 and Torture 102.

My mother managed not to lose her mind. She also managed not to lose her soul. She did not sell herself to the enemy for a loaf of pumpernickel, a can of sardines, a chocolate bar, a kiss, fleeting love, or survival. But she survived. Some neighborhood girls, rich or poor, it didn't matter to them, single or married, because that didn't matter either, frequented the barracks and took part in the rituals of life. Sitting on the soldiers' laps, they flirted and carried on and wore their helmets because it made them feel very important. They thought that the war would never end and that their carousing and flirting with the enemy would go on forever. And if the war did end some day, the enemy would rule and they would rule as well. They were on top of the world. Some of the women even wore the German uniform. They had become or thought they had become German soldiers, having more or less joined the German Army. They walked on the streets surrounded by the men in uniform and everyone around them had to make way. One day my mother was walking down the street in Piraeus. Two soldiers were coming from the opposite direction and in their midst were two women--a mother and a daughter whom my mother had known on the island. Both women were dressed as soldiers. They did not look my mother in the eye. The men, however, did. My mother moved aside to let them pass. As she did so, she glanced at one of the men. Years later, she remembered his eyes. They were not human.

She relied on her writings to help her pull through. Every night she would put on paper all of the day's political events and her emotions regarding the war, all in verse. By the end of the war in 1945, she had a seventeen-page book which I have saved in the bank vault and which I plan to publish eventually. It is my mother's masterpiece that I admire. I have learned many things from it. She kept it in her suitcase on her voyage to this country. A bottle of Greek cognac which she also had in the suitcase, cracked, soiling the cover and the first few pages of her book. To me, it is symbolic. It reminds me of the trials and tribulations my mother went through in her motherland, in her new country, and in her life in general. However, she finally prevailed. The last part of her book is in perfect condition.

I never had a childhood. Although I had many toys and cannot be classified as "deprived", I was lacking in other things. Despite my mother's love and attention, I felt alone, poor, and miserable. But I put on a front and did not share my pain. I camouflaged it. Just like the color black. Black is one of my favorite colors. Besides being a sexy and mysterious color, it, too, is the color of pain and it camouflages it. But as a toddler and as a child, my favorite color was yellow. Yellow. Because it's sunny.

I often think of Demeter, the goddess of the harvest. She had one daughter who was her sunshine and whom she adored. Persephone's father is Zeus himself but it is Demeter who raises her. Being a single parent is not easy. It takes its toll. When Demeter was distraught at her daughter's misfortune, she neglected the Earth. It went dry and just stopped producing. The foliage did not bloom. People were starving. My mother worked very hard. She worked as a seamstress, as a baby sitter, and as a cleaning lady. She did all this so that I should not want.

What is a sacrifice? Judge for yourself.

Chapter Fourteen

Rainbow, Rainbow*

This is a story for all the children in the world. May your precious little lives be as sunny as the sky on a beautiful day and may your dreams blossom like the flowers in a colorful garden.

After it stopped raining, the flowers in the field looked up at the sky but did not like what they saw. They were used to seeing the sky laugh after a downpour and now they could not understand why the sky was so sad. Every time after it rained, Apollo, the god of the sun, would make his appearance in all his glory in his golden chariot, holding his horses' reins in his hands. He would travel across from one end of the sky to the other. But now, the flowers saw nothing.

"Please, sky, make the sun come out. Make the earth laugh," the flowers called. The sky tried. He sent the clouds to look for the sun but they could not find it. The sky called to the moon: "Did you, by any chance, see the sun, my little moon?"

"Where would I find the sun?" replied the moon. "I don't even know what the sun looks like. You see, Mr. Sky, I have never met the sun. But I will tell you a secret. Artemis, the twin sister of Apollo, is hiding among the thick pines and cypresses in the forest, a little further away from here. Surrounded by her faithful hounds, she hunts for hours as she carries her quiver full of arrows on her shoulder. She runs after the deer and the fowl that inhabit the forest. Ask her. She will tell you."

The sky looked down at the earth. He heard the barking of dogs. He looked more carefully. Boy, he thought, the moon was right. Artemis, in all her majesty, was so involved in her hunt that she did not even notice the sky looking at her.

"Goddess Artemis," the sky called. "Where is your brother? Why is he hiding?"

Artemis was startled. She was not used to being spoken to when she was hunting. Fierce and unstoppable, she ran after her prey and never missed her aim. She still remembered vividly the incident with her mother. When Leto was on her way to Delphi to visit Apollo, the giant Tityus tried to harm her. Nothing could stop Artemis. She took an arrow from her quiver, set it on the bow string, pulled, and let the arrow fly. Whoosh! It flew across the forest, hitting Tityus. He dropped to the ground, never to see the light of day again.

She looked up at the sky. "Let me tell you, Father Sky," she said. "My brother thinks the flowers do not love him."

The flowers held a meeting. They called Demeter who knew what it was like to lose a loved one. Pluto, god of the Underworld, fell madly in love with Demeter's daughter, kidnapped her as she was gathering flowers in a field, and took her with him to be his queen. Because she ate six seeds of a Chinese apple that Pluto fed her, she had to spend six months of the year with him and six months with her mother. The flowers hoped Demeter would help them. After all, she was the goddess of the harvest and, without the sun, her crops would not grow. Demeter thought and thought. Then she made a suggestion. Each flower would send the sun something beautiful and special; something of itself....

A red peony was in full bloom in one part of the field. It sent the sun a red petal full of love.

An orange-spotted tiger lily decided to send its orange hue.

Some blades of green grass growing in a field sent their love, hoping that the sun would like their gift and come out once again. A few blades of grass flew up to the sky. The three-leaf clovers sent the sun plenty of good luck.

What beautiful gifts for the sun! Such colorful and happy gifts!

The yellow daisies were exceptionally happy. They were just as yellow as the sun. They sent the sun their yellow petals and knew that he would really like their gift.

A little further away, some jasmines were spreading their fragrance all around. That's exactly what they sent the sun--their fragrance.

Oops! Demeter realized, a little too late, that the jasmines should have sent the sun their petals. Their purple petals to make the sun happy. What could everybody do now? They all looked around. They looked and looked. They thought and thought.

Suddenly the sky was filled with swallows. The sky was filled with pigeons, with robins, and with doves. Of course, they would know what to do. "Guess what?" they all cried. "In that valley below, We saw purple amaranths growing next to purple hyacinths. Ask them to send the sun their hues."

The amaranths and the hyacinths heard the birds. They were very angry. "No!" they called out. "We will not send the sun our hues. We will keep our colors for ourselves. We do not want to share."

Demeter heard what the amaranths and the hyacinths said. She got very upset. She ran to find her daughter and asked Persephone to help. These flowers all loved her because she was a queen, and purple was the color of royalty. They understood each other. Persephone loved them very much, too. She loved all the flowers growing on the earth. "I will speak to them," she told her mother.

When the amaranths and the hyacinths saw her coming near them, they all felt bad. They were ashamed. Persephone, the daughter of a goddess and of Zeus himself, looked radiant. She was absolutely beautiful. The flowers just could not say no to such a beauty queen. So, they sent the sun their purple hues.

Demeter and Persephone looked up at the sky. All the flowers looked up at the sky, too. What do you think they saw? The sky was all lit up! The sky was so bright! The earth was happy, too. Wait! Wait! What was that? Something that looked like the hoofs of horses began to make an appearance in the sky. The flowers, the grass, the three-leaf clovers, Demeter and Persephone could not believe their eyes. Slowly, slowly, there appeared four beautiful, well-groomed horses kicking their legs, prancing around, kicking their legs, neighing happily, and oh!....pulling something. Yes, the beautiful well-groomed horses were pulling something. But what were they pulling? It looked like a chariot. A chariot! A chariot that was carrying Apollo, the sun god. But wait! There was more! What was Apollo guiding? What was that? It looked like the sun. It was the sun. Here comes the sun! Yes, here comes the sun! Riding in his chariot, Apollo was guiding his horses and carrying the sun across the sky. The sun was smiling. The sun was very happy. The sun was very happy and it was surrounded by beautiful hues. The sky was smiling. The sky was very happy. The sky was very happy and it was surrounded by beautiful hues. All these hues formed what seemed to be half a circle in the sky. What exactly was it? Was it half a circle? Wait! Wait! It was a rainbow! The sun and the sky were surrounded by a gigantic, happy, colorful rainbow. This rainbow was made up of all the colors and all the gifts that the flowers and the grass had sent them as gifts.

---

* My passion for Greek mythology was instilled in me by Mrs. Effie Callas (Kalogeropoulos), an elderly neighbor, who baby-sat me in my tenement in the Garment District. Through her narrations, I was transported to Mount Olympus, the home of the Greek gods and goddesses. To Mrs. Callas, I was the little grandchild she never had. I never got to meet my grandmother on the Greek island. Mrs. Callas took her place. Mrs. Callas was like a grandmother to me. It is to her memory that I dedicate this short story and the Greek translation that follows.

ΟΥΡΑΝΙΟ ΤΟΞΟ

Σαν έπαψε η βροχή, τα λουλούδια στο λειβάδι κύτταξαν τον ουρανό εκεί ψηλά, μα δεν τους άρεσε αυτό που είδαν. Μαθημένα να βλέπουν τον ήλιο να γελά έπειτα από την μπόρα, τους φάνηκε παράξενο που τώρα ο ουρανός ήτανε λυπημένος. Μετά από την βροχή, με όλη την μεγαλοπρέπειά του, ο αφέντης του ήλιου, απάνω στην χρυσή του άμαξα και κρατώντας τα ηνία στα χέρια του, ο θεός Απόλλωνας παρουσιαζότανε ταξιδεύοντας από την μία άκρη του ουρανού στην άλλη. Μα τώρα, τίποτα.

«Σε παρακαλώ, ουρανέ», φώναξαν τα λουλούδια. «Κάνε τον ήλιο να παρουσιαστή. Κάνε την γη να γελάση.» Ο ουρανός προσπάθησε. Έστειλε τα σύννεφα να τρέξουν να τον βρουν, μα τίποτα. Ο ουρανός φώναξε το φεγγάρι.

«Μήπως είδες τον ήλιο, φεγγαράκι μου;» ρωτά ο ουρανός. Μα πουθενά δεν τον είχε δει ούτε και το φεγγάρι.

«Πως να τον δω τον ήλιο σας;» τον ρώτησε αυτό «Αφού ποτέ δεν τον αντάμωσα. Ούτε και που τον ξέρω. Θα σου πω, όμως, ένα μυστικό», είπε το φεγγάρι στον ουρανό. «Εδώ πιο πέρα, στο δάσος, στα πυκνά εκείνα πεύκα και κυπαρρίσια, κρύβεται η Άρτεμης, η δίδυμη αδερφή του Ήλιου Απόλλωνα. Περιτρυγυρισμένη από τα πιστά σκυλιά της, με την φαρέτρα της στον ώμο και τα τόξα της στο χέρι, κυνηγά ώρες ολόκληρες τα ελάφια και τα πτηνά του δάσους. Ρώτησέ την. Αυτή θα σου πη.»

Ο ουρανός κύτταξε κατά γης. Άκουσε γαυγίσματα. Κύτταξε πιο προσεχτικά. Καλά τα είπε το φεγγάρι. Η Άρτεμης, αφοσιωμένη στο κυνήγι, δεν είδε τον ουρανό να την κυττάζη. «Θεά Άρτεμη», φώναξε ο ουρανός.

«Που είναι ο αδερφός σου; Γιατί δεν φαίνεται;» Η Άρτεμης ταράχτηκε. Δεν ήταν μαθημένη να της μιλούν όταν εκυνηγούσε. Άγρια, ασταμάτητη, αλαφιασμένη, έτρεχε πίσω από την λεία της και ποτέ δεν έχανε τον στόχο της. Στην μνήμη της πολύ νοερά ήταν ακόμη η μέρα που όταν η μητέρα της η Λητώ πήγαινε στους Δελφούς να επισκεφθή τον Απόλλωνα, ο γίγαντας Τίτυος προσπάθησε να την χτυπήση. Οπότε η Άρτεμης, αβάσταχτη και χωρίς να χάση τον στόχο της, πέταξε το τόξο της και άφησε τον Τίτυο νεκρό κατά γης. Κύτταξε τον ουρανό εκεί ψηλά.

«Να σου πω, Πατέρα Ουρανέ», του είπε. «Ο αδερφός μου νομίζει πως τα λουλούδια δεν τον αγαπούν.»

Τα λουλούδια φωνάξανε την Δήμητρα. Η θεά ήξερε από χαμούς. Κάποτε όταν η κόρη της εμάζευε λουλούδια σε ένα ανθόσπαρτο λειβάδι, ο θεός του κάτω κόσμου την απήγαγε για να την κάνη γυναίκα του. Εξ'άλλου, η Δήμητρα ήτανε θεά της φύσης και των σπαρτών. Αυτή θα βοηθούσε σίγουρα γιατί χωρίς τον ήλιο, η γη δεν θα'ταν πια γεμάτη χόρτα και φυτά.

Η Δήμητρα εσκέφθηκε και τελικά πρότεινε κάτι πολύ πρωτότυπο. Θα έστελνε το κάθε λουλούδι ένα δώρο για τον ήλιο, κάτι από τον εαυτόν του. Μιά κόκκινη παπαρούνα ανέμιζε εκεί κοντά. Έστειλε στον ουρανό για τον ήλιο ένα πέταλο κόκκινο γεμάτο αγάπη. Ένας κρίνος ποικιλόχρωμος δέχθηκε να στείλη την πορτοκαλή του όψη. Τα πράσινα χορτάρια θα έστελναν κι'αυτά μερικά κομμάτια από το λειβάδι για να ευχαριστήσουν τον ήλιο και να τον παρακαλέσουν να φανερωθή. Μαζί με τα χορτάρια, τα τυχερά τριφύλλια φωνάζανε να στείλουνε κι'αυτά την πράσινη όψη τους για το γούρι του ήλιου. Τι ωραία δώρα για τον ήλιο! Όλα χαρούμενα και γελαστά. Οι κρίνοι, ειδικά, καμάρωναν γιατί όταν αυτοί θα έστελναν το δώρο τους στον ήλιο, αυτό θα του έμοιαζε πολύ. Κίτρινοι σαν τον ήλιο όπως ήταν, θα είχε ιδιαίτερη προτίμηση γι'αυτά. Πιο πέρα στο λειβάδι ένα μάτσο γιασεμιά σκορπούσαν την ευωδιά τους πέρα για πέρα. Αυτήν ακριβώς έστειλαν στον ήλιο. Μα, για σταθείτε. Κάτι έλειπε. Το μωβ! Η Δήμητρα σκεφθότανε, σκεφθότανε. Τι να κάνουνε τώρα; Πως να συμπληρωθή το όμορφο μπουκέτο;

Εξαφνικά ο ουρανός γέμισε χελιδόνια. Γέμισε περιστέρια. Αυτά θα'ξεραν ασφαλώς. «Είδαμε στο λειβάδι,» είπαν αυτά, «κάτω εκεί στην ρεματιά, κάτι ωραία ζουμπούλια!»

«Δεν δίνουμε!», φωνάξανε. «Δεν δίνουμε στον ήλιο!»

Η Δήμητρα φώναξε την κόρη της. Η όμορφη Περσεφόνη έτρεξε να δη. Την αγαπούσανε αυτά όπως και 'κείνη αγαπούσε το κάθε φυτό της γης. «Θα τους μιλήσω εγώ,» είπε. Τα ζουμπούλια σαν την είδαν, ντροπιάστηκαν. Αυτή, σαν κόρη θεάς που ήταν, με πατέρα τον Δία, έλαμπε και σκορπούσε την ομορφιά της στ'απέραντα της γης. Τα ζουμπούλια δεν μπόρεσαν να αρνιθούν μπροστά σε τέτοια χάρη. Έστειλαν στον ήλιο κι'αυτά τα πέταλα τα μωβ τους.

Η Δήμητρα μαζί με την Περσεφόνη κυττούσανε τον ουρανό. Μαζι τους, όλα τα φυτά που είχανε στείλει τα δώρα τους στον ήλιο κυττούσανε τον ουρανό. Και τι να δουν; Έλαμπε, έλαμπε ο ουρανός. Έλαμπε, έλαμπε η γη. Σιγά–σιγά, πρόβαλλαν τέσσερα άλογα. Σιγά–σιγά, πρόβαλλε η άμαξα του Απόλλωνα. Πρόβαλλε και ο ίδιος κρατώντας τα ηνία. Μα τι ήταν αυτό; Γύρω από την άμαξα, γύρω από τον Απόλλωνα, ήταν ο ήλιος γελαστός. Ήταν ο ήλιος γελαστός περιτριγυρισμένος από όλα τα δώρα που του είχανε στείλει τα λουλούδια, περιτρυγιρισμένος από ένα πολύχρωμο ουράνιο τόξο.

Chapter Fifteen

Tug of War

The ancient Greek tragedians and Greek mythology have covered it all--from infidelity, to jealousy, to passionate love, to unrequited love, to retribution. Let's not forget the Oedipus and Electra complexes. Sibling rivalry ranks up there along with rage, competition, brainwashing, cannibalism, homicide, infanticide, and matricide.

Passionately in love with Jason, the barbarian princess Medea is influential in his acquiring the Golden Fleece. For him, she forsakes her homeland. For him, she kills her brother and strews his pieces into the sea on her way to the ends of the earth with Jason.

Her antics do not stop there, however. Betrayed by the ungrateful Jason, she offers his mistress a beautiful robe only to have it cling to her skin and burn her alive. She forgets her maternal feelings and slaughters her children in her attempt to hurt and humiliate Jason, leaving him desperate and devastated.

Aristotle summed it up nicely when he preached that wherever there is friendly competition, there one will find progress. What was that about friendly competition? It depends on the competition. There was nothing friendly about Medea and Jason's mistress. Furthermore, it can be friendly as long as one of the contestants does not happen to be a deity. Fantasy is an important element in Greek life, you see.

Speaking of competition....I am reminded of Arachne who claimed that she was extremely better at weaving than the goddess Athena who happened to be "the master" when it came to arts and crafts. Bitterly insulted, Athena challenges Arachne to compete. Arachne complies and, through her tapestry, portrays the interaction of the gods and goddesses with the humans. Angry at not finding a flaw in Arachne's works, Athena sprays her with hell-bane and Arachne weaves eternally while hanging. Thus, Athena avenges herself in front of the horrified villagers and clears her soiled reputation.

Greek mythology gives a reason for what the ancient Greeks did not understand. It fascinates the readers as well. It has even penetrated the English language. Narcissus, a golden-haired youth, falls in love with himself upon seeing his refection in a river. Not realizing the situation and unable to fulfill his desire, he pines away. From his name, the English language is richer by one word.

Speaking of riches....

When Agamemnon, King of Mycenae, was fighting in Troy and undoubtedly looted, plundered, pillaged and raped, he was cuckolded by his wife with his cousin, no less. Upon his triumphant return, Clytemnestra and her new partner Aegisthus murder him. Electra, appalled and devastated at the death of her extremely beloved father, vows revenge. How she worshipped her father! She waits patiently for the return of her exiled brother Orestes and together they execute their mother and stepfather. Electra, however, unable to get over her father's death, mourns for him day and night, day and night, until she drives herself into a frenzy. And she mourns and mourns and yearns for him. And languishes. Electra and her complex emotions perplex her even more.

And then there is Oedipus. Who can forget Oedipus? Oedipus who unknowingly slays his father and marries his mother. Riding on horseback and coming from opposite directions, both men encounter each other on a narrow road. Neither one yields the right of way. Oedipus slays the other rider because Greek blood reaches the boiling point very fast. Laertes falls because he quickly forgot the oracle that had predicted precisely the meeting that took place. Both men are victims of their stubborn Greek genes. Each had to be the victor because each had to be the victor. How typically Greek.

In literature there is such a thing as "fictional realism". According to literary experts, any human being who exemplifies traits and performs actions as any particular character in literature, is said to be a perfect example of this. In other words, incredibly, a character from a paper page comes to life right in front of your eyes.

Methinks I saw....Oh, well!

One day, he announced, "Find me a wife!" Almost everybody in the tri-state area grabbed a lantern and went looking for a suitable female for his princeship. Lantern, you ask? Well, in ancient Greece, the cynical philosopher Diogenes walked through the streets of Athens, lantern in hand, looking for an honest man. However, this one was looking for the perfect woman, whatever that might entail. And yes, I got ideas. Maybe I qualify. Why not? You never know.

The first meeting took place. He didn't move my heart strings but I decided to give him a chance, if he agreed. He informed me that 700 females had made an attempt to get to know him. Speaking of conquests. However, the biggest conquest of all was being approved by his dearly beloved mother. This was like climbing Mt. Everest barefoot. And surviving to talk about it. Now, that's a conquest. Gasp, gasp. Was he looking for a wife? Get real! Anyway, one must be given a chance. After all, he is highly educated and his pockets are bulging. Oh, is that a hundred-dollar bill I see that just dropped out of his pocket? Wow!! There's plenty more where this came from. Thank goodness for pre-nups. Okay....

"So, what exactly are you looking for, Dr. Money Bags?" I heard me ask. (The names have been changed to protect the jaded.) I used to be so timid....

"Someone as nice as you."

Did he mean I qualify? Did he approve? If he did, that was half the battle. Wow!!

What now remained was winning over the Matriarch. That would be like Sisyphus in Hades pushing the heavy, humongous rock up a hill only to have it roll back down once it reached the summit. Here it goes again....Keep trying!

This one is not good enough. That one is not good enough. The other one is not good enough. Is that what he thinks or is that what Jocasta, oh--I meant is that what Mama thinks? There is always something wrong with every candidate.

"Who's this?" her Majesty screamed in my ear every time she picked up the phone. Who was I? After a while I didn't know nor did I care. It is a blur. I do not know who I am. I am not deaf. Ouch! Oh, now I am.

"I'll call you."

"I'll call you."

"I'll call you. One day this week, I'll call you." So many promises. "Maybe we can have lunch together one day this week. Give me your number." Again.

He must have told me ten times. And every time he lost my number. Freud would be having a field day. Thank goodness I didn't wait for him to feed me. I'd starve to death.

"He's not home. He's out for the evening," the Matriarch informed me on another occasion. Yeah, right. Or was he? Maybe. Let's not accuse. Now, now, let's not jump to conclusions.

Male chauvinist pig. That reminds me of Circe. Mysteriously hiding in the wilds of East Africa, she was surrounded and protected by cannibalistic guards who defended her fiercely. Exotic, voluptuous females waited on her hand-and-foot. Their being deaf-mutes further guaranteed that her secrets were safe with them. She had beaten the effect of time With her magic potions. She evaded death and waited to be reunited with her reincarnated lover. Despising men, she transformed lost, unfortunate sailors into swine. However, she had the honor of meeting Odysseus, the Sailor of all sailors. Odysseus was the only man who intimidated Circe. Following Hermes's advice, Odysseus raised the wand the winged god had given him and stood up to the cruel sorceress who, until that point, had treated herself to cholesterol loaded breakfasts. Bacon and eggs, anyone? Commanded by Odysseus, Circe turned all the pigs into the men they used to be. Speaking of men....

What am I getting into? Do I really love him? Love him?!! I don't even like him. What is it now? Tug of war? Gee, this umbilical cord is awfully strong. Too strong, if you ask me. If I only had a scissor....Now, now, let's not get carried away.

I call again.

"He is not here. Is this Fay?"

"Yes, it is. We had agreed for him to pick up a plant."

Speaking of roots.

"Just a second." She mumbles something that I do not understand. To whom is she speaking? Mumble, mumble, grumble, grumble. "He is not interested in the plant, dear. Give it to someone else."

This is called communicating thru a medium.

I didn't know what to think. Was this her response or his response thru her? I pursued the hidden truth. To him it was a conquest. I was conquest number 701. Dr. Oedipus had found a wife. He had her all along but did not realize it. A match made in Heaven.

And they lived happily ever after, I'm sure.

Chapter Sixteen

The Glory That Was Greece

The ancient Greek philosopher Socrates believed that even teachers learn. They learn from their students. The marketplace where the philosophers and men in general congregated to discuss and dispute issues was off limits to women. Only the women whose vocation it was to please the men would frequent the agora. As a matter of fact, that is where Pericles, the statesman of Athens during the Golden Age of Greece, met his mistress Aspasia. She caught his attention because she not only had charm and a way with men, she had a brain as well. She could converse with the opposite sex as well as they could converse with each other. From then on, Pericles and Aspasia became an item. The closest I ever come to being in the company of Socrates is when I visit Athens Square Park in Astoria, the park I was instrumental in building as a legacy to Hellenism. I was the English secretary of the Athens Square Park Committee for five years. At that time, I was teaching both Greek and English in my school. I got my Greek students involved in the project. Together, we worked to maintain our heritage. The bronze and copper solid statue of Socrates beckons the crowds. I stand in front of him and am literally transported to the Athens of 2,500 years ago. I see myself wearing beautiful, flowing robes and sandals on my feet. My hair is up in Grecian curls. If I could turn back the clock....

It is the holiday season of 1980. I am standing in the middle of the dance floor of a prestigious New York City hotel. It is a few days before Christmas and the band is playing lively Greek music. The crowd is in a festive mood. We each reach into a box designated by gender and pull out a piece of paper on which one pair of names is written. We begin to search for the mate whose name is part of that pair. Thais and Nathaniel. Who is Thais? She should be seeking Nathaniel. By the same token, Nathaniel should be seeking Thais if, hopefully, the same pair of names was picked from the box designated for the men only.

It is 356 B.C. Olympiada, former Princess of Epirus and wife of Philip the Second, is awaiting the birth of their son. She has had a strange dream. In her dream, she was holding a thick twig, flames shooting out at both ends. However, the twig was short. One of the high priests was summoned to interpret it. The son she is carrying is destined for fame and glory. He will conquer the West; he will conquer the East. But he will live a short life.

Alexander the Great conquered the world as far east as India. He conquered North Africa. He was a terrific strategist. He calculated everything with mathematical precision and never lost a battle. He befriended and treated the enemy with respect. He married the Persian Princess Roxanne. He ordered his men to marry Persian women.

Alexander the Great died of a high fever in Babylon at thirty-three.

Thais....married to Nathaniel. She was drawn to Alexander and became his mistress. Thais, wife of Nathaniel and courtesan to Alexander the Great.

Egypt....Ptolemy the First is in power. Pharaoh of the land.

Ancient Greece. The Far East. Egypt.

Thais and Nathaniel.

Thais, Nathaniel, and Alexander.

Sometimes, destiny does things that man cannot explain. How and why some things happen is inexplicable. And yet, Alexander the Great met Ptolemy, and yet, Thais met Ptolemy as well.

Thais, Nathaniel, Alexander, and Ptolemy.

Thais, wife of Nathaniel and courtesan to both Alexander the Great and Ptolemy the First of Egypt.

Nathaniel was not at the holiday celebration. Thais was crestfallen. Alexander the Great was seeking his Roxanne. But on the other hand, why should Thais be crestfallen? With Alexander and Ptolemy as her lovers, what did she have to fear? Obviously, there was a pattern here. Thais was drawn to men of power.

Men of power. Pericles. Alexander the Great. Ptolemy the First of Egypt.

Achilles.

Sometimes destiny does things that man cannot explain. How and why some things happen is inexplicable.

Thetis, daughter of a lesser god, married Peleus, the mortal Peleus, who had killed his brother. The gods were horrified. They placed a curse on the marriage. Even before Achilles was born, his parents knew that he would live a short life. His parents knew that he would live a short life because Thetis had been told by an oracle.

Without Achilles, the Greeks could never win their battles in the Trojan War. He was the best warrior the Greeks had. The enemy froze at the sight of him. Yet, not even the double-breasted armor that Hephaestus made for him at the request of Thetis was enough to protect the Prince of the Myrmidons. Paris, Prince of Troy, son of Priam and lover of Helen of Sparta, shot the fateful arrow that pierced Achilles in his heel and brought on his demise. The Greeks tied his corpse on a horse and led it to battle. Dead or alive, he instilled tremendous fear in the enemy. It was the daring of Achilles, his fierceness and his fearlessness, that contributed to the Greeks winning the war, bringing glory to themselves and to the Greek city-states.

Troy fell in the year 1190 B.C. Achilles died at thirty-three.

For some inexplicable reason, there is a pattern here. The parents of Achilles and Alexander the Great knew that their sons would die young. They had been forewarned in some way. Both men were of royal birth. Both men were warriors. Both men died at thirty-three.

Diogenes.

A cynic philosopher who slept in a gigantic jug. Could he explain the ironies of life? Who knows? Why did he sleep in a jug?

Extravagance was unnecessary. One day, he saw a young boy approach a public fountain. The boy used his cupped hands to carry the water to his lips. Diogenes immediately discarded the cup he carried tied to a string around his neck, considering it a luxury. He proceeded to drink the water the samee way the boy had done. The basics were enough.

Alexander the Great was going through Athens with his entourage. He saw Diogenes sleeping in his jug and approached him. Alexander offered to give Diogenes anything he asked for. Diogenes looked up at him and asked him to move out of his way as Alexander was blocking the sun: "Do not take from me what you cannot give me." This was his reply. Alexander was taken aback. He had not given Diogenes the sun; he could not take it from him.

I have a small alabaster statue of Diogenes on my bookcase. He is holding a lantern in his hand. There is a dog at his feet. He is going around Athens looking for an honest man. Will he find him? I do not know. In the meantime, he has his faithful dog to comfort him.

Euclid.

One of the greatest mathematicians of all time and a contemporary of Alexander the Great and Ptolemy the First of Egypt. He had the great honor of being invited to Egypt by Ptolemy to teach mathematics in Alexandria.

There is a pattern here. All three men know strategies and the power of mathematics and numbers. All three men know the many mysteries of the world. All three men know that the many mysteries of the world relate to mathematics.

It is April of 1989. I am at an Athens Square Park dance in one of the catering halls in New York. The room is crowded with Greeks who are there in support of the project--the park that will serve as a legacy to Hellenism for the generations to follow. I am going around selling raffles. The prizes are magnificent and represent Greek art and culture. I buy raffles as well. You never know. I am left holding the last raffle from my roll. It is only just this one. How can I sell it? Who will buy just one? I decide to buy it myself.

The prizes are raffled off. One of them is an alabaster statue of Nike of Samothraki and another of Socrates. There are beautiful pieces of pottery. The final prize is a bust of Alexander the Great. His head, covered with his wavy hair, is leaning to the East as it rests on a heavy wooden stand. It is leaning to the East from whence the sun rises; to the East that he conquered; to the East where he spread the civilization of ancient Greece in all its glory.

I won that prize. The statue of Alexander the Great became my possession. It rests on my mahogany armoire in the bedroom. It symbolizes my heritage. It reminds me of the warrior who spread civilization and of his influence on the world. It reminds me of his love and respect for everyone regardless of background. It reminds me of his love of learning. I am an educator. I respect learning. I try to instill in my students the beliefs of Alexander the Great.

A statue of Athena stands by the main entrance in Athens Square Park. One arm of the statue is extended as if beckoning the crowds, welcoming them. Ever since the time of the Olympian gods, the Greeks have been hospitable to friends and strangers alike. Athena is welcoming the crowds to the park, to our past, to our legacy.

It is the present. It is the past. It is the future. It is all one and the same. The philosopher Spinoza used to say that everything connects. The philosopher Spinoza used to say that everything is one and the same.

Chapter Seventeen

A Trivia-l Perspective

You see things your way; I see things my way. Just exactly what does all this mean? You are entitled to disagree. But when you do disagree, are you absolutely certain? Certain of what? Certain of what you see in front of you? Certain that what you see is that which everyone else sees? I don't know--it is very confusing and uncertain. Uncertain? That brings me to the "theory of indecision and doubt". I see a piece of blue material. How deep is the blue hue? How light is the blue hue? I see what I see. What do you see? I know what I know. Actually, I don't know.

Picture this: a bedroom with the bed's headrest against the wall, a mirrored dresser opposite the bed. Picture perfect and balanced. But not to the Chinese. Why not? It drains the couple's love, they say. You open up a store where a flower shop once stood. No good. No good? Why not? The roots of the flowers, the essence of the roots, the spirits of the roots, will suck the success right out of your business. They will drain it. They need nourishment and that nourishment will come right out of your profits. Now, if you open up a restaurant or any other store where a bank used to be, your profits will be huge. The spirits will abound and will bless your business. Money will become money.

In China, there is a flower that blooms only at night. It is "tan hua". It is a beautiful, fragrant white flower that is found nowhere else on earth. Why is it found only in China? I do not know. What makes it bloom at night instead of during the day? I do not know. Nobody knows.

The Chinese are not fond of clocks. The ticking of the clock and the movement of the clock's hands serve to remind them of the passage of time and of the impending end. Half a world away, Edgar Allan Poe presents the same theme in his short story **The Masque of the Red Death**. The revelers, having been secluded in a huge castle by their friend Prince Prospero in his attempt to cheat the Red Death that has been devastating the country, are reminded of the passage of time every hour on the hour. When "the ebony clock" chimes away, the dancing stops. The musicians stop. The elder members wipe the cold sweat from their brows. It is amazing how the two cultures share the same perspective.

Red is the color that symbolizes happiness--to the Chinese. At the birth of a son, the proud father distributes red eggs to celebrate the event, as opposed to an American proud father who may give out cigars. In Chinese homes, red banners are hung to ring in the New Year. Red symbolizes new beginnings, happiness, life.

To a Korean, red symbolizes death. He never signs his name in red ink for if he does, he signs away his life.

Everything is a matter of perspective.

Numbers--mystical, a code, a symbol, a message

Picture this: the number 8 on a piece of paper
Which end is up? It does not matter. Horizontally, is it the same?
Horizontally, it is the symbol for infinity.

Picture this: the number 6 and the number 9
Upside-down their value changes. Which is right? I do not know. I do not know because everything is a matter of perspective.

What does the number 17 mean to you? To an Italian it means death. Yes, that's right, death. The Roman numeral for seventeen is XVII which is an anagram of VIXI which means "I have lived, hence I no longer live, hence I am dead". There is no seventeenth floor in an Italian building; there is no table seventeen at an Italian affair. There is no thirteenth floor in an American building; there is no table thirteen at an American affair. For the Hebrews, however, the number thirteen is a very lucky number.

Everything is a matter of perspective.

Shakespeare wrote seventeen comedies. Hamlet ruled Denmark for seventeen years. Jacob lived in Egypt for seventeen years. Joseph was seventeen when he was sold by his brothers. America began her war for independence in 17-76. The Irish celebrate St. Patrick's Day on March 17. Can you think of anything else?

What would you consider an appropriate bridal shower gift? How about a table setting for four? That is a perfect gift. What is a perfect American family? A family of four. Right? Right. There are four sides to a square, four sides to a rectangle, four sides to a trapezoid and four sides to a sheet of paper. Without paper, there would be no books; without books there would be no knowledge; without knowledge we would still be in the Dark Ages. To the Japanese, the number four is not a lucky number. To the Japanese, the number four means death.

Everything is a matter of perspective.

When the Greek city-states were at war with the Persians, the Persians sent a messenger to King Leonidas of Sparta to ask for water and earth. The king decoded the cryptic message as: "Give up your homeland" and responded accordingly with his famous: <Μολών Λαβέ>. "Come and get it." Many years later, Dionysios Solomos who wrote the Greek national anthem stated: <Χωρίς πατρίδα δεν ζει ελεύθερη ψυχή.» "Without a country, a free soul cannot live."

Everything is a matter of perspective.

When I was a student in college, my philosophy professor lectured on many subjects. He pointed out certain things that make me think. The message was that everything is a matter of perspective.

The spring and summer months for us in the Northern Hemisphere are March through the end of September. When the earth blossoms and we are enjoying the fragrance of the flowers, the Southern Hemisphere is experiencing rain, snow, and low temperatures. In Australia, the earth blossoms in the month of December. Is that wrong? What is right? When should the flowers bloom? When should the snow fall? Who is to say what is right?

Everything is a matter of perspective.

The Greek alphabet consists of twenty-four letters and Greeks read from left to right. The American alphabet consists of twenty-six letters and is read from left to right. The Hebrew writing is read from right to left. The Chinese read from top to bottom. Who is right? What is right? I do not know.

Everything is a matter of perspective.

Life is a matter of perspective.

The ditty I was taught by my kindergarten teacher opens the door to serious discussion.

"Row, row, row your boat gently down the stream, Merrily, merrily, merrily, merrily, life is but a dream."

My professor discussed serious issues. What is life? Is being awake really a dream and when we are "awake" are we really not? Do we experience actual life when we sleep and dream? Who is to say? I do not know. The German philosopher Goethe said, "Of all Peoples, the Greeks have dreamt the dream of life best." I don't know about that in regard to the Greeks, but I do see a similarity between my professor's words and Goethe's words. Did Goethe think that life is really a dream? In the book Kapetan Mihalis by Nikos Kazantzakis, the Cretan rebels find themselves drinking in a cemetery along with the keeper of the grounds. One of the rebels raises his wine glass and makes a toast: "To the health of the dead." That is exactly what he says. Does this mean that the "dead" are really alive someplace else and truly experiencing life? Does this mean that we, here on earth, are the ones who are not really alive? I do not know. What is the right answer to this? Nobody knows.

Everything is a matter of perspective.

I see my image in the mirror. I raise my right hand but I see that I am raising my left hand. I raise my left hand but I see that I am raising my right hand. I see my image in the mirror. Who is that in the mirror? Who is that in front of the mirror? What is going on behind my mirror? Can the person behind my mirror see me and what is going on around me? I do not know. How many of me are there? Is that another one of me? Is that an illusion of me? I do not know.

Everything seems so real. I think I am in front of my mirror. I am getting confused. What is right? I do not know.

Everything is a matter of perspective.

Is this chapter in my book a good enough chapter? Is this chapter in my book mentally stimulating? Am I writing my next book? Am I actually sitting here in front of my computer and typing down all my ideas? Am I actually really here? Am I actually anywhere? I do not know.

Everything is a matter of perspective.

Chapter Eighteen

Transformations

Oh, the fragrance around me is wonderful. Trees and more trees. Fresh green blades of grass, some of them wild, growing any which way. Bushes and more bushes. A tall, handsome cypress tree on my left and a beautiful coniferous tree on my right. Nature at its best. Boy, look at those gorgeous cones. Oops!! One cone just dropped to the ground. My neighbor sees the cone drop from her branch and turns to me and winks. Boy! I'm such a lucky oak tree. She noticed me. I can't believe it. You know, I'm not so bad myself. I may be three-hundred years old, but I look great for my age. I don't apply any make-up the way some of you humans do. All I need is an adequate ground water supply for the major part of the year and I'm okay.

My ancestors have been on the earth since the Paleozoic Age. That's when all the dinosaurs were roaming the planet. Some of my relatives became extinct during the Jurassic Period, but hey, things happen. Then other trees grew in their place. And now, here I am. Move over world, here I come and here I am. Just look at my acorns! I have so many, I don't know what to do with them. No other tree around me is more prolific. Guess what? That makes me the dominant species of the area. Wow!! Oops!! There goes an acorn. There goes another one. Hey, what's going on?

You know, I am not only handsome, I am also very valuable. I take in carbon from the air. That's my staple diet. The carbon dioxide combines with the water in my leaves and it becomes oxygen. And I give out this oxygen so that you humans can survive. There are so many rings in my trunk. Sh!! If anyone were to count the rings, he would figure out my age. Oh, that's right. I did tell you that I am three-hundred years old. My beautiful neighbor is making me flaky. Well, I can't help it, I'm only human--what am I saying? I mean, I'm only a tree. Trees have feelings too, you know. Let's get back to me. As I was saying, I am very valuable. I help to sustain life on earth. As for my acorns, the squirrels eye them continuously. Occasionally, I drop a few pounds. I mean--a few acorns for the squirrels.

Let me tell you a little about my family tree. Oops!! Pardon the pun. I meant to say my relatives. I have relatives all over. My gnarly cousins grow near deserts. Sometimes they grow near grasslands. Oaks like me, firs, and chestnut trees grow in high mountain areas. My beech and maple relatives reside in the Northeastern part of the United States. My cousin the Southern Magnolia is truly a Southern belle. She makes the family proud. I don't see her because she lives in Louisiana and Mississippi. And then there are my brothers. I have many brothers near the Great Lakes. They are equally generous with their acorns. I know because we oak trees are very giving. And they are handsome, just like me.

Did I tell you about my bark? My outer bark is made of inactive cells that form protection for my inner bark. It's like you humans with your outer layer of skin and your inner layer of skin. My inner bark carries food made in my leaves downward to my storage cells. As for my roots, they absorb the food elements found in the soil. They absorb the food through my tiny root hairs. I just love spreading out my roots. That's what gives me this great straight posture and makes me look so young. That's right--so young. I have relatives that are as old as one-thousand-five-hundred. Yes, that's years. You see, we trees are blessed with longevity, thank goodness.

Who *is* that? I hear voices. *What? Mountain climbers?* How did they get so high? Boy, these humans, I'm telling you, they can be so annoying sometimes. I hope they see how handsome I really am. Oh, they are getting closer. Wow! There are women among them. Don't these women have anything better to do than climb mountains? They are so adventurous!! Oh, here they come. HEY, HEY, DON'T STEP ON THOSE ACORNS!! I DROPPED THEM FOR THE SQUIRRELS. Funny, they don't pay attention. Are they *deaf*, or *what?* Am I not making myself clear? It's as if they can't hear me. Boy! Those two look like they're in love. Just like me and my beautiful cone cutie here. Oh!! They're approaching me. What's he looking for? *What? A penknife?* HEY, MISTER, WHAT DO YOU THINK YOU'RE DOING? DON'T WRITE ON MY BARK!! YOU ARE WRITING ON PUBLIC PROPERTY!! THIS IS CALLED DEFACING PUBLIC PROPERTY!! What is he carving? It feels like a heart. What's he carving *now*? What's *this*? Initials? HEY, DON'T PUBLICIZE YOUR LOVE ON MY BARK! Teenagers!! Oh, but these are adults. HEY, MISTER, HOW WOULD YOU LIKE IT IF I WROTE SOMETHING ON *YOUR* FACE? HOW ABOUT I SCRATCH *YOUR* FACE WITH ONE OF MY BRANCHES? WOULD YOU LIKE THAT? *NO, I DON'T THINK SO.* GEE!!

Oh, I just love it here high up on this mountain with the other trees all around me. I really get along great with my neighbors. Whoosh! Hey, what was *that*? Oh, *gee*, it's that majestic eagle again. I can't understand why he has to fly so low over my top here. Every time he wants to fly above the clouds when it rains, he takes this route. He hates rain so he flies over the clouds to get away from it. HEY, PAL, CAN'T YOU TAKE ANOTHER ROUTE? YOU ALWAYS BRUSH UP AGAINST MY HAIR, OH, I MEAN AGAINST MY UPPERMOST BRANCHES AND LEAVES. CAREFUL!! I DON'T WANT YOU BREAKING ANY OF MY BRANCHES!! Eagles hate the rain and they are the only birds that can fly above the clouds. So what?! Does that make them special? I don't *think* so. I think oak trees are *more* special. So there!!

Oh, here comes that forest ranger again. There's a botanist with him. I know what they want. They want my sap. They want to tap my handsome bark and get the liquid that is in there. And you know what? Some of it will be made into gum. That's right! Don't tell me you don't chew gum when you want to rest, relax, and unwind. Oh, I'm getting so carried away. Part of me may become paper. It's something like cloning. I said *something* like cloning, but not quite. I will exist in a different form. I am so great! You know, the word "paper" comes from the Greek word papyrus. The ancient Greeks knew papyrus as early as the beginning of the 5th century B.C. I'm so smart!!

Gee, where am I? Oh, oh, oh, I'm so ticklish. This pen on my face is really tickling me. What is it writing? *What*? *An essay on the history of papyrus?* What is the title of the essay? Wow!! The Invention of Papyrus. Boy, that pen is writing about me right on me or right on me about me. Ha, ha!! I'm so clever. I just like the way I speak. How do you like my play on words? If there's a lot to write, there will be writing on my back as well. I just hope that later the essay will be written on the blackboard there for everyone to read about me. I am so important. Look at that. I wish cone cutie were here to see this. She would be so proud of me. This whole essay will be about me. Wow!!

HEY, KID, DON'T DO THAT!! HAVE SOME RESPECT FOR PUBLIC PROPERTY!! DON'T YOU KNOW YOU CAN'T WRITE ON

THE DESK? WHAT'S THE MATTER WITH YOU? HOW WOULD YOU LIKE IT IF I WROTE ON *YOUR* FACE? WOULD YOU LIKE THAT? *I DON'T THINK SO*. Gee!! Oh, here comes another character. HEY, I'M NOT A CHAIR!! GET YOURSELF OFF MY FACE!! DON'T SIT ON MY FACE!! WEREN'T YOU KIDS TAUGHT ANYTHING AT ALL? Oh, thank goodness, he got up. What is it with these kids? They just weren't taught respect. OH, NO!! Here comes another one with a pen in his hand.

HEY, I HOPE YOU'RE NOT THINKING OF WRITING ON MY FACE LIKE YOUR FRIEND HERE JUST DID!! WHAT ARE YOU WRITING? THIS IS NOT NICE. BEHAVE YOURSELF!! WHAT ARE YOU WRITING? OH, NO!! WHAT ARE YOU WRITING? OH, NO!! SUCH LANGUAGE!! WHAT DO YOU THINK THIS IS? PAL, THIS IS A *SCHOOL*, NOT THE *GUTTER*!! Boy, some people were not taught respect. SO, DO YOU FEEL BETTER NOW THAT YOU DEFACED SCHOOL PROPERTY? HUH, *DO YOU*? TELL ME, DO YOU FEEL BETTER NOW THAT YOU GOT ALL THAT OUT OF YOUR SYSTEM? GEE!! You know, I'm still handsome despite all that. I'm still useful despite my old age. Three-hundred years old and still going strong. I've been everywhere. I've seen it all.

What's that I see on the floor? That's odd. What's that on the window sill? That's odd, too. Is there a parade going on that I don't know about? Is some ethnic group celebrating anything? What *is* this? YIPES! YIPES! DON'T TELL ME! I CAN'T BELIEVE THIS! IT CAN'T BE!! IT CAN'T BE HAPPENING!! TERMITES!!!! TERMITES!!!! HEY, KID, SEE THAT CAN OVER THERE? GET THAT CAN OF SPRAY!! QUICK!! HELP!! HELP!! HEY, KID, GET THAT CAN OVER THERE IN THAT BACK CORNER OF THE ROOM!! QUICK!!

Chapter Nineteen

Dear Toula Column

Dear Toula,

About six months ago, I met this great guy at work. He asked me out and although he is not Greek, I took him up on the lunch date. We hit it off right away and we are now seeing each other on a steady basis. The problem is, my Greek father does not know about this. He gave his Greek friend his word that I would marry his son, who happens to be a doctor. Nobody asked either of us and I do not like this other guy. He does not care for me either. Officially, I am engaged, according to my father. Don't my feelings count? Please tell me what I should do.

Distraught in Astoria

Dear Distraught,

You should sit down and have a serious conversation with your father. He should realize that this is not the Greek village and this is not how things are done in America. Women have rights. They can date anybody they want and they certainly should have a say when it comes to choosing a life partner. The fellow should do the same with his father. Good luck with your one-on-one.

Toula

Dear Toula,

I have a very serious problem. I am twenty-two years old and I am not allowed to date. I don't see any harm in going out to dinner or to a movie with a guy. My Greek father says that dating is for "loose girls". He says the right thing to do is to get engaged and go to dinner with my fiance. Please tell me what to do because I feel so constricted here.

Rapunzel

Dear Rapunzel,

You should try to speak to your father so he could win your trust. Explain that all you want to do is go out to dinner with the young man. There is no harm in that at all. Ask your date to come to the house to pick you up so your father can speak to him and hopefully get to like him.

Toula

Deerr Tula,

Me Grreek fatherr Repoonzel. Me no care what you say. Me boss my house. No you. Everybary my house listen to me. Me no wan my gerl en estreet with everybary. Go to restoran with guy no good. Me tell you why because no good. No good because efter dinner baklava and kataif. Plenty sweet. Efter dinner, how you say? Deezert.

Mr. Patroklopoulos

Dear Toula,

I have been dating a nice Greek boy for two years. The problem is that in all the two years that we have been dating, he has not made any moves. He tells me his mother tells him if he does anything with a Greek girl, she will kill him. He says Greek girls are sacred. I liked him from the very beginning and now I am crazy about him. I can't take it anymore. What should I do?

Snow White in N.Y.

Dear Snow,

This is absurd. If he cares for you as well, he should consummate the relationship. Even if he doesn't care for you, he should still consummate the relationship being that a man is a man is a man. In the meantime, get him psychological counseling and play it cool. One more thing--change your image. Maybe you remind him of his mother.

Toula

Dear Toula,

I have been married to my Greek husband for thirty-five years. I cook, I clean, I wash his clothes, I raised our children, and I am a faithful wife. In all the thirty-five years we have been married, he has never told me he loves me. Whenever I ask him if he does, he answers with, "I married you, didn't I?" Whenever I try to tell him I love him, he waves his hand in the air and says, "Okay, okay." Deep down I know he loves me but it would be nice to hear it as well. How can I get him to tell me even once?

Waiting to hear it

Dear Waiting,

Some men have difficulty expressing their feelings in words. Instead, they may buy their wives beautiful gifts or take them out to dinner. If your husband is the type that has difficulty, it is better not to press the issue. As long as he is a good husband and father, then let it suffice. Greek men in general have difficulty saying those three little words. It is not in their genes.

Toula

Dear Toula,

I read yesterday's column and I recognized my wife's complaint. I married her, didn't I? Is that not an indication? She wants to hear it. Hear what? Nonsense! I am a man. I am a Greek. A Greek is very proud. He does not become emotional. Period. Case closed.

Unemotional

Dear Unemotional,

Your wife deserves the Nobel Peace Prize.

Toula

Chapter Twenty

Greek Correspondence

My Dear Husband Dionisi,

    I know you will find this strange. I have a need to speak with you but I do not have the courage to do so. I am therefore turning to my writing skills. Please do not be angry with this but I need to convey certain things that have been bothering me for a very long time. I was brought up in a Greek household and was taught to keep my opinions and ideas to myself. This is why I am having difficulty speaking up.

    When we were going out, you took me everywhere. You loved going to the Greek night clubs and you used to tell me that you and Zorba have the same ideas about life. "Life is too short; it is to be enjoyed," you would say. You would throw plates on the floor in the night club and break them. Your excuse was that this is how a Greek expresses his enthusiasm. Many Greeks around us in the club were doing the same thing. However, you do the same thing at home. You throw plates on the floor and against the wall and break them. You do not take me anywhere anymore.

    When we were going out, you wore such a fragrant cologne. I became drunk with desire but would not tell you because I was so embarrassed. Now, you don't wear it anymore; you don't even wear deodorant.

    You don't tell me you love me. You never did tell me you love me. I don't know why you married me. I am very confused.

    I will be at my mother's this afternoon if you should want to call me. If not, I will be home in time to make dinner and to iron your blue shirt for you to wear tomorrow to the Greek soccer game.

Your wife,
Ermione

Ermione,

What *is* this? Something *new*, that you have to write me a letter and I should sit down like a fool to answer it? Well, only because you promised to iron my blue shirt for me to wear to the Greek soccer game. I break plates in my house because I am a MAN. Because I am a MAN, I do anything I want in my house. I have to make my presence known and I have to get my point across. What is this nonsense about my cologne? I don't remember wearing any cologne. Are you getting me confused with some other man? You mean to tell me that when I was taking you out to all these Greek night clubs you were also dating another man? So how come you didn't marry *that* one? I don't wear deodorant because not wearing deodorant is manly. Yes, to smell of sweat is manly indeed. Oh, and what is this further nonsense about love? Why do I have to tell you I love you? I *married* you, didn't I?

Your husband,
Dionisi

P.S. Ermione, twenty years from now, I can only picture myself with you. It is your hand I want to hold when I am dying. It is your image that I want to close forever in my heart.

Dear Cousin Argyri,

I hope my letter finds all of you in the best of health. We here in the Greek village are fine and send you our regards. Just to keep you up-to-date as to what is happening here, I want to tell you that Yianni finally asked for Maria's hand in marriage. You remember Yianni, don't you? He used to ring the church bell on Sundays and holidays, and whenever there was a happy or sad occasion. He still does that but now he also chants during the service on Sundays and I have to tell you, he has quite a voice. He was in love with Maria for ten years but was too shy to speak to her father. Can you believe that? He is not rich but Maria's father is giving them that house they own at the foot of the mountain near the wheat storage bin. It needs renovation so they hired Kosta and his men to do the work. I passed by on my donkey the other day and that place is beginning to look pretty decent now. The tiles on the roof were chipped and whenever it rained outdoors it also rained indoors. I heard that Maria's father bought imported Italian tiles for the roof. Can you believe that? Imported Italian tiles! Anyway, the wedding is set for the following Sunday. The entire village is going to the wedding. Each of us is bringing a dish of some sort. Diamanto is going to make makaronada. I just love the way she makes that dish with the chopped meat, tomatoes and bechamel sauce. You know, I married a good woman. She cooks, she cleans, she sews, and when it is necessary, she helps me in the fields. The fence around my hen house had ripped in some places and someone went in during the night and stole a couple of my chickens. I had to go to the neighboring village to buy wire so that I could repair it. Diamanto and I worked on it together and now it is as good as new. So, tell me, are you going to come to the village to visit? We now have bus service from town twice a week. Let me know. My regards to your wife and family.

Your cousin,
Mitsos

Dear Cousin Mitso,
I hope my letter finds all of you in the best of health. We here in New York are fine and send you our regards. Just to keep you up-to-date as to what is happening here, we bought our airplane tickets for our trip to Greece. We will be flying either out of Kennedy or La Guardia on Olympic one of these days and we should be in Athens either next week or the following week. I don't know exactly when because it really does not matter. When we are in Athens, we will be staying in one of the hotels for a few days because the wife wants to take in some of the Athenian sites. We will be coming to the village some time after that, either on a weekday or on the weekend. Now that I have finalized our plans, please make sure you meet us at the village bus stop.

Your cousin,
Argyris

Dear Cousin Argyri,
I hope my letter finds all of you in the best of health. We here in the Greek village are fine and send you our regards. We were so happy to hear that you and your wife will be coming to the village to see us. Don't worry, we will meet you at the village bus stop. I will not hear of it. I insist.

Your cousin,
Mitsos

Dear Mana,
This is your son writing to you. I just want to tell you that I am sending you and my sister Asimina a package. The package contains material for you so that you can sew a nice house dress for yourself. I am also sending you a set of towels for Asimina's dowry. The set of sheets I will send at a later date.

This way, when Asimina gets married, she won't have to buy any bed and bath accessories. In the package you will also find coffee beans, Lipton tea bags, Vick's cough drops, Bayer Aspirin, Wrigley's chewing gum, and that's all. One more thing, when you open the bottle of aspirin, you will find in it a $100 bill. Let me know when you get the package.

Love,
Your Son

My Dear Son,

This is your mother writing to you. I got your letter a while ago and not long after that we received your package. The material you sent me is absolutely beautiful. I will start to make my house dress one day this week. Asimina loved the towels and she wants me to ask you to send her one more set. This way, she will keep one set for her dowry for when she gets married and the other set of towels she will keep for her daughter's dowry, in case she has a daughter. We got the coffee beans and I will grind them, make coffee, and think of you when we are drinking it. The Lipton tea bags I will save for emergencies. Whenever we get a sore throat, we will drink tea. We will quiet the cough with the Vick's cough drops and decrease the fever with Bayer Aspirin. The Wrigley's chewing gum I will give to the neighborhood children. The $100 bill should help us pay for the wood that will keep our fireplace blazing during the freezing winters of the northern Greek villages. You also wrote that you were sending us that's all. I looked and looked in the package but I did not find anything. Are you sure you sent it? Let me know because I am worried. I hope it didn't get lost. Take care of yourself.

Love,
Your Mana

Dear Neighbor in the City,

I hope my letter finds all of you in the best of health. We here in the village are fine and send you our regards. I want to share with you something I heard on the Greek news. I wonder if you heard.... There was this plane coming from somewhere and it was heading I don't really know where. Well, it crashed and I have no idea how many people were killed. Did you, by any chance, know anybody on that plane? Please write to me and let me know.

Your village neighbor,
Antonis

Dear Village Neighbor Antoni,

I hope my letter finds all of you in the best of health. We here in the city are fine and send you our regards. I was surprised and pleased to hear from you. I think I heard about that plane that was coming from somewhere. So, you heard about that too, eh? It is amazing how news travels fast and so accurately, especially in the Greek village. Antoni, tell me, are you my neighbor Dino's son or my other neighbor Dino's son? Write to me as soon as you can.

Your city neighbor,
Spiros

Dear Spiro,

I hope my letter finds all of you in the best of health. We here in the village are fine and send you our regards. In answer to your question, yes, I am you neighbor Dino's son. Be well.

Your village neighbor,
Antonis

Dear Cousin Kosta,

I hope my letter finds all of you in the best of health. We here in Athens are fine and send you our regards. It has been quite a while since I have written and I know that you were asking about my family. Well, let me tell you the latest.... My wife Stasa is a very good wife. She takes excellent care of me. We celebrated her nameday on Greek Easter Sunday, being that her full name is Anastasia. All five of our boys were here with their families and we had Easter dinner in a restaurant in Athens because we now live in a condominium and cannot roast the lamb like we used to do in the village. You know, my five little boys grew up, went to school, graduated, met nice Greek girls and got married. I have five sons. Can you believe that? All five carry the family name. There's more. My oldest boy Thanos, who has my father's name, has three children. His oldest child, a boy, is named Mitros, after me. So the child's name is Mitros Thanos Papalexandrakis. You know how it goes--the child always uses his father's name after his name so that people should know whose son he is. My second boy Petros has a son. His name is Mitros Petros Papalexandrakis. Manolis, my third boy, luckily, has a son whom he named Mitros. So, that child's full name is Mitros Manolis Papalexandrakis. Are you counting? So far, there are three grandchildren named Mitros. My other son's wife gave birth to a girl first. We were all devastated. How could she do that? How could that happen? Well, the child is named Anastasia, after my wife. Their second child is a boy, thank goodness. Guess what? His name is Mitros Alexis Papalexandrakis. You guessed it....He is the son of my son Alexis. And my youngest son Tasos, well, he also has five boys. Is that a coincidence, or what? His oldest boy is named Mitros Tasos Papalexandrakis. When their children grow up, they will carry on the tradition of the family tree and the importance of names. Someone told me your news. Is it true you have three girls? GIRLS??!! What's the matter with you? What kind of a man are you? What happened? Who will carry on your family name? This is terrible. Well, as the Greek expression goes, it's all in the stars. Send me pictures of the family. Take care of yourself.

Your friend,
Mitros Thanos Papalexandrakis

My Dear Son,

I am writing to you in America and I hope that my letter finds you in the best of health. As for me, my son, my health is getting worse. My vision is decreasing. It is with great difficulty that I am writing to you now. Your sister Maria took me to Athens to see a specialist but he said that there is nothing he can do. I also developed heart trouble since your father died eight months ago. My strength is going. I can feel it. I know I don't have much longer. I am writing to you to beg you to come to the village so I can see you one more time before I die. It has been twenty-five years since I saw you last. I remember the day you left our village as if it were yesterday. I came down to the harbor with you to see you board the ship. I stood there for hours waving my white handkerchief long after the ship had sailed away. I stood there praying that you should have a safe trip and that you should be well in that strange, foreign country. My son, you have not set foot in our village since that day. I sent you two letters before this one but you did not respond. I don't know what the problem is. Did you not get them, perhaps? I do not want to die before I see you one more time. Please consider making the trip so that I can die happy. Even if you do not come, I want you to have my blessing.

With all my love,
Your Mother

May, 1945

My Dear Sister,

The war is finally over. Now that the mail can go through once again, I can write you a letter, not knowing if you are still alive. I have a lot to tell you. It has been five long years and I truly hope that you are all well.

We here on the island are trying to pick up where we had left off but it is very difficult. There is much devastation. Many of our loved ones are gone. Our home is destroyed. When they bombed the churches on the island and the church of St. John fell, the tremor knocked down the walls of our house. Remember how we could hear the priest chanting the liturgy? From our courtyard we could see the bell tower. We are now staying in one of the houses by the steep incline, Katarrakti, you know, the incline that leads to the uppermost part of the island. Ah, our beautiful island that is shaped like a crescent. If you take certain turns, you will reach the houses on the other side of the crescent. Ah, our island with the houses situated amphitheatrically. Well, the owner of the house we are staying in said we can do so rent-free as long as we maintain it. She is leaving for Piraeus so things sort of worked out. It is a two-level house. One door faces the incline and another one faces the alley on the other side. It is not our house but for the time being it will suffice. We are grateful that we are allowed to live in it. Very few houses suffered minimal damage and this is one of the few. The walls of most houses are gone, and some walls are left standing only a few feet high. Windows have been knocked out and everything looks forbidding. What an awful sight!

It is very difficult to rebuild as no one has much money. With the economy being what it is and with the value of the drachma having been divided in half during the war, no one has much. Has that helped the government? I am not sure. Do you know what that meant? We had to save twice as much to buy what we wanted. Of course, there was a lot of smuggling going on and things were sold on the black market, at least that is what we heard. All I know is that the value of money went down during the war and now I have to work very hard.

I always tried to get some of the American cheese and powdered milk that UNRA sent, not for me, mostly for Mother. That meant waiting on long lines but I didn't care. The British soldiers got to know me and some of them met Mother and when they saw me on line they gave me chocolate bars to bring home to her.

Thank goodness I have our sewing machine, you know, the Singer sewing machine I bought in 1930. I did not sell it during the war because I knew I would not be able to make a living if it all ever came to an end. This is what sustained us before the war; this is what will sustain us now. Before the war I had my customers from Rhodes. You remember, my Jewish customers who ordered embroidered tablecloths, sheets, pillowcases, and aprons. They sent me good money. Well, all that is gone. They are gone. Yes, they are all gone. I am so sorry. It breaks my heart.

I did not use my sewing machine during the war. To survive, I got up at three every morning and went to the mountains around four with some of the neighborhood women to pick dandelions to sell. We also gathered twigs and sold those, too. It was very dangerous because there are a lot of mines all over, but we tried to be careful. That is not all. One day when we were ready to start on our return trip, packs and all, a German soldier appeared out of nowhere and was coming toward us. I felt my knees shake because he was approaching me. The other women ran off and left me standing there all by myself. He came up to me very close, put his rifle to my temple, and asked me if there were British soldiers hiding in the basement of a church on the mountains. I told him there were not. He took a few steps back, started to leave, and came up to me again, putting his rifle to my temple one more time. By then, I was so scared I couldn't see straight but I told him there were no British soldiers anywhere. He lowered his rifle and went off. That left me pretty shaken. As for my friends, well, they were nowhere in sight. We still go for dandelions and twigs but no one discusses anything. It is as if none of this ever happened. But that's okay.

I am very tired. I am tired of the hard life I have had. When there was a raid, I grabbed Mother and carried her on my back as we, with many of the islanders, headed to the mountains for safety. You know, they did not bomb up there. One night, some of our neighbors and cousins left for Anatolia in their boats. We did not want to go. It does not matter. Those who went to Palestine are now coming back and they tell us how everything there was plentiful during the war. They were taken care of very well.

Anyway, let me tell you something--one day, before our house fell, I went to visit one of the neighbors and when I returned there was a German soldier standing in the middle of our courtyard talking to Mother. She told me that he had asked for water. I glared at him and told him to get out. He looked at me and just stood there. I meant what I said. I told him to get out of our courtyard. Without a word, he made an about-face and he left.

Let me tell you what happened to Vanessa--you know, you baptized her son. She had been washing clothes and opened her door to throw out the soapy water. An Italian soldier coming down the incline slipped on the suds. Yes, the island is full of them and many of them have defected as they do not want to fight anymore. He was defecting, too. Well, one of the grenades he was carrying exploded, injuring him and Vanessa. Shrapnel became embedded in her leg and she was crying out for dear life. Her family ran to call Doctor George. I went to see her. Because she was so seriously injured, he called two British doctors for consultation. Yes, there were British on the island. As a matter of fact, they had turned many church basements into armories but I dared not tell that German soldier when he asked me. He would have killed me on the spot and they would have gone looking for the British to kill them. Anyway, it was decided that Vanessa be transported to Cyprus. While Dr. George was consulting with the doctors, German planes were heard flying overhead. The British doctors ran to the window to see what was happening and raised their rifles to shoot. Dr. George begged them not to for there would be retaliation. When he realized that the planes were circling his clinic, he turned to Vanessa and told her that she had saved his life. His clinic was destroyed. The patients and their visitors were all killed. The doctor's sisters ran down the incline, distraught at the thought that they had lost their brother. But they had not. Instead, he was in the house tending to Vanessa. This is what I call cheating death. He did not go to the clinic; he went elsewhere instead. Had Vanessa not been doing the wash and not thrown out the suds when she did, had the Italian soldier not been coming by when he did, the doctor would not be here now. Is this a strange succession of events, or what? Vanessa just returned from Cyprus the other day.

Nothing is the way it used to be. Everything has changed. Our house needs repair. Even though the walls have been knocked down to some extent, the stone staircase in the courtyard, that same staircase on which our grandmother and her mother used to tread, that staircase that led up to the two bedrooms, stands unharmed. The top landing is still there but it only leads to a wall whose windows have been knocked out. The grapevine that Mother planted when she was pregnant with you dried up. Do you remember how it used to hang over the wall of our courtyard, the wall that enclosed our house from the alley? All the neighbors used to come and pick grapes. Whenever they wanted to make stuffed grape leaves they would come and pick all the leaves their hearts desired for they were plentiful and Mother and I didn't mind. The other day Mother asked one of our neighbors by our house to give her a root of her vine. It seems that Mother had given her a root from our grapevine a long time ago to plant. Well, she did, and it took. Now she gave Mother a root from that. Mother will plant it one more time in its original place in hopes that it will grow. It is very important to Mother that she do this. It does not matter that it will grow in a courtyard with a house that barely stands. Mother will nurture it. She will water it. It will grow again and it will blossom.

We think of you in Piraeus. It has been ten long years since we have seen you. I still remember the day we all came down to the harbor with you when you were leaving in search of a better life. I can't forget the hard life you, too, had on the island. You started to work at the age of nine. You had to drop out of school after the fourth grade and you gave up your dream of becoming a teacher. You stayed up all night mending fish nets. I remember standing next to you holding the oil lamp to help you see what you were doing. You also learned to sew and to embroider. You used to make a lot of money sewing for the Italians who were here before the war broke out, when our island and was under the Italian occupation. It is unbelievable how our island and the neighboring islands went from being under the Turkish yoke to the Italian yoke, beginning in 1912. The Italo-Turkish War was a war not very many people know about, lasting only a very short while. It is unbelievable that we are still under the Italian occupation. Anyway, you used to make shirts for the Italians and for other men as well. I remember when you embroidered a white linen tablecloth along with the twelve napkins to match. It was a very important job for you, asked of you by a woman whose husband had a municipal position on the island. He worked with the Italians. She was going to have one of the Italian Commandantes and his entourage for dinner and she asked you to monogram the tablecloth and napkins, and on every corner you made sure you included the letters ML. She was so pleased, she paid you well. But this was not enough. Opportunities like that did not come by all the time. You wanted something better and you left. You left and now we have not seen you in all of these ten years.

Oh, my sister, I hope that you are well. We have been hearing stories about the horrors of the war and everything that happened in Piraeus. We heard about the air raid sirens and the bombings and about the ship that exploded in the middle of the night after being bombed. We heard about the famine and the filth and the lice. We want to hear from you. We want to get a letter from you telling us that you are well. Every day Mother waits for the mailman to come by to ask him if there is a letter from you. Perhaps now that the war is over, you will come to the island to see us for a short while. Mother misses you terribly. Save your money and make the trip. It is only nineteen hours by ship from Piraeus. As for me, I will look for new customers who want embroidered goods. Maybe I will get some from Rhodes once again. In the meantime, I will clean houses. I will whitewash their walls and I will make a living. Life is hard, my sister. We love you very much and we miss you very much. Mother sends you her love and so does everybody here on the island. Take care of yourself.

With love,
Your younger sister Anna

Chapter Twenty-One

A Journal

My Dear Journal,

Today I turn eighteen. I am not happy as should be expected of an eighteen-year-old whose whole life is ahead of her. Instead, I have a pit in my stomach and a pain in my heart. I am writing to you under the bedcovers for fear of being seen by father. I will hide you somewhere so that no one will be able to find you, my dear journal.

There is talk of my marriage. Marriage to whom? I do not know anyone nor do I care for anyone. I had dreams. Dreams of going to the city to study at the University. But they were dashed by father. He says that only boys should go to the University. The girls should stay home and learn the tasks of the housewife. I was taken out of school at sixteen and since, I have learned to cook and clean. I have learned to weave on the loom. I have woven blankets and rugs. I have woven rugs whose colors and threads reflect the brightness of the sun and the warmth of nature. I have woven covers for the sofa and the beds. Fiery red covers that reflect a heart kindled by the arrow of the god of love. Eros evades me. But even if I were to be struck by one of his arrows, what good would that do? I dare not express anything of the sort in this household. I am tired. I get up at the crack of dawn to take the woven blankets to the river to wash. I am tired of pounding the blankets with the paddle. Then I carry them home and lay them out in the sun to dry. Oh, my dear journal, I am afraid. Afraid that I will be forced to marry as did my older sister. Forced to marry a man I neither know nor love. What can I do?

My older sister is unhappy. But she stays married. She has no other recourse. She tells me that this is what I have to do. It is what every respectable

Greek girl does. Mother cannot defend me. She also is obedient and servile. She tells me it is the destiny of the female children to always do as they are told. I used to play school when I was a child. I would roll up my light summer blankets like cigarettes and, with my pencil, I drew eyes and eyebrows, a nose and a mouth. I made believe they were my dolls. I taught them many things. I asked them questions and they answered them. I wanted to be a teacher. I used to be so happy!

Last week, I went to the river to wash the clothes. I heard a horse galloping in the distance. I heard it coming nearer. When I looked up, I saw a stranger on horseback just looking at me. He pulled the horse's reins and the animal approached. He asked me if I could direct him to the nearest village. He looked very stern and cruel. I gave him directions to our village. He pulled the horse's reins again and off they went. My stomach turned and my hair stood on end. I did not get a good feeling. I returned to the house and did not have energy for anything.

There is talk of my marriage. Father talks of my marriage.

Your eighteen-year-old friend

Dear Journal,

Today I visited grandmother in the village. She spoke to me of many things. In the past, she hardly spoke to me of her youth and of her past but today she did. It made me feel so good. I felt so much closer to her. I know she is lonely since grandfather passed away last year, but what can she do? Mother asked her to come and live with us but she is used to her village. She says she cannot get used to a strange place whose villagers she does not know. Although, it would not be the first time she would be doing such a thing as grandfather took her from her village to his when they were newlyweds.

Newlyweds....Grandmother spoke to me of the time she was a girl in her village and of the time she was preparing for her wedding. She was not in love with my grandfather. That's right. Grandmother told me she was in love with someone else. He would pass by in front of their home on horseback just to look at her. She told me that he was crazy about her blonde braids and the way she would swing her head, her braids flying this way and that. He could see the ocean bottom in her big, round, blue eyes. He whispered all that in her ear whenever no one was around. She was sixteen years old. She was sixteen years old but has never forgotten. She remembers his every word. She wanted to marry him but he never proposed. Never proposed. Maybe he just didn't propose in time. That she cannot remember.

Her father chose a man for her. He told her that she would be getting married the following Sunday and that she would see her husband in church on the day of the wedding. Grandmother started to cry. She told her father she could do no such thing. Her father picked up his rifle and put it to her temple. He said her refusal only meant one of three things--either grandmother was in love with someone else, or she had lost her chastity, or she had no inclination for the opposite gender. He asked her which of the three was the one that applied to her. The following Sunday, my grandmother married the man her father chose. When she first saw him in the church, a terrible feeling came over her. She feared him. This is what she told me. Her father told her she would eventually get over it and that she would learn to love him. This was her father's answer in the church on her wedding day.

The day after their wedding, he brought her to his village. They were married sixty-two years. They had five children together. She told me many things. I did not ask her if her father's prediction came to pass. I did not ask her if she learned to love my grandfather.

Your sixteen-year-old friend

Dear Journal,

I do not know where to begin. I am nearing the end of my life. However, I remember the years of my youth, when my life was just beginning, as if it were yesterday. I got married at eighteen. My husband was twenty-two. He was very handsome. He had straight, dirty blonde hair and an air about him that is hard to describe. He always told me that he loved me and complimented me. He claimed he was crazy about me.

When we were married for six months, his two older brothers in Brazil wrote to him, asking him if he would go there to work in the mines. They promised him good money. Life was hard here in the village. We didn't have much money but we had our love. I begged him not to leave. He promised me that he would only stay there for a year and that he would come back to me full of money and dreams for our future. What could I do? One morning, he took the path down the mountains to the city. From there he would go to Piraeus to board the ship for foreign ports. Before he left, I hugged him and I kissed him and he told me I was a fool. I was foolish to cry and act like a child. He told me that these tears, my tears, would turn into one big smile upon his return. He promised to come back to me.

The months went by. At the end of the year, he did not mention coming back. His two brothers could not take life in the mines anymore and returned to the village and to their wives. My husband stayed. The first few months, he wrote to me. Then his letters became fewer and fewer and more far apart. I was left without money. I had to depend on the charity of his two brothers. What could I do? I could not work.

I waited for him every day. I looked on the far horizon and wondered where he was and what he was doing at that particular moment. I often wondered if he was thinking of me. I waited for a letter. I waited every day for mail. Nothing came addressed to me. No letter came from him.

The years went by. My brother insisted I forget about him and that I should remarry. It is not easy to forget a man you love so much. I always thought he would come back. And then what? What would I do then? I never loved another man. I never knew another man. It is not easy for a woman to just pick up and go on.

I had our wedding picture on the wall. I looked at it, I looked at him, and felt his presence in the room. After a while, when twenty years had gone by, I would look at the picture and not recognize the girl I saw. How could that girl be me? I did not look like her at all. The twenty years became thirty and the thirty became forty. I never loved another man.

The years went by. One morning I looked in my mirror and thought I saw my grandmother. I did not recognize the woman whose reflection I saw. I did not recognize my white hair on my head or the wrinkles on my cheeks. I did not recognize me. I counted the years. It did not seem so long ago. I did not realize seventy years went by. I did not know if he still lived. I did not know if he had died. How could I know?

But life holds many surprises for us all. Two days ago, I saw the mailman coming up the slope. It did not startle me in any way for I was used to his coming to bring various mail. However, the closer he got, the more I realized that he was holding an envelope that looked so strange. I saw it had a foreign stamp. I held my breath. It could not be! No! Not a letter from him! Seventy years! You mean he was still alive in Brazil? Oh, my goodness! My heart began to race the way it did when we first met. My heart began to race the way it did when he used to take me in his arms and whisper sweet nothings in my ear. It could not be! But it was! A letter from him, from Brazil. I held the envelope in my hands and kissed it. I held the envelope in my hands and kissed him. It was a letter from my beloved husband. I never loved another man.

"My dear wife", it began. My heart began to race. Then I read on. I had to sit for fear of losing my balance. I had to sit in order to continue reading his letter. Years ago, he had met someone?

Another woman in Brazil? A Brazilian? How long ago? Seventy years? That could not be. What was he saying? What did he want? He lived with her and together they had five children. What? Five children? How can that be? He thought of me, he said, occasionally and always wanted to come back but you know how things are. One thing leads to another and another and another and nothing ever goes back to how it was back when. Now he was very sick. He was on his death bed. He was afraid to die. He was afraid to die without asking me to forgive what he had done. He wanted his soul to leave his body easily. If I forgave him, he said, he would know even if I didn't write because he would die peacefully. Because he would not suffer. His soul would not get caught between his tongue and teeth. If I could not forgive him, he would understand. He would understand because he caused me so much pain. I hugged his letter in my arms. I brought his letter to my heart and held it for a long time. I could not believe that he was still alive after all these years. I held his letter in my arms and looked up at the sky. "Oh, my dear husband," I said. "I forgive you with all my heart." I know he had an easy death. I know because I felt it in my heart, in my soul, in my entire being.

Marigo

Dear Journal,

I am of Greek descent. I am of Greek descent but I did not marry a Greek. I did not do what a nice Greek girl would do but I do not regret it. Deep in my heart, I know I did what was right for me. My story is unusual. It starts when I was seventeen.

My parents were very rich; so rich, in fact, that we would go on vacation every year. We went on trips abroad. My mother really had no responsibilities around the house. The servants took care of that. She would meet her friends for coffee and for a game of cards. I was raised by a governess. I was tutored at home by the best tutors my father's money could buy. My father was in the tobacco business. He had workers in the fields to plant, to cultivate, and to pick his tobacco. They rolled cigars. They rolled cigars and shipped them to ports around the world. The money would come pouring in. The money would come pouring in like the rain pours from the clouds when the sky cries because the sun decides to hide.

The summer of my seventeenth birthday, my father announced that we were to go to an exotic land. That's what he called it--exotic. We would go for two weeks, take in the sights, and return to our town in time for me to pack my things and leave for the University abroad.

I fell in love with Egypt. I fell in love with the palm trees, with the white sand, and with the pyramids. I was fascinated with the five-thousand-year-old structures. I was awed with the Pyramid at Giza, one of the seven wonders of the ancient world. I did not want to leave. Mother said I was being ridiculous and that I behaved this way everywhere we went. I laughed. I looked out the window of our hotel room and could see nothing but sand on the horizon. Something caught my eye. Something that moved from one end of the horizon to the other.

I had not seen anything like that before except in books that spoke of cultures other than my own. A caravan on the desert. I wondered. One of my tutors had told me that a camel can walk on the desert for days without drinking a drop of water. He told me that a camel spits and that when it does, the spit travels for miles and may end up hitting a person in the face as he would be walking on the street or in the square. I did not know what to believe.

I fell in love in Egypt. I did what another Greek girl would not have done; I did what was forbidden and what my parents frowned upon. I loved an Arab boy. Ali was tall and thin. His black hair was straight, as opposed to my thick, curly hair that became so wiry every time it rained. His eyes were dark and deep. When I looked into his eyes I saw the stars; I saw the sky. I saw the love he had for me. The love for me that summer of his twentieth birthday. I fell in love with Egypt and Egypt fell in love with me. My parents threatened to disown me; his parents threatened to disown him. My parents left without me. I have not seen them since.

Ali and I got married. Twice. One ceremony we had for me. Another ceremony we had for him. And nobody converted. We had respect for both our faiths. On his high holy days, he went to the mosque. He celebrated the way he had been taught. On my high holy days, I went to church. I celebrated the way I had been taught. But there was one thing--the children. He raised the children in his faith and I respected that. It did not bother me at all. The way I saw it and still do, everything is one and the same. It may go by a different name, but it is still one and the same. We never had an argument. He never raised his voice at me. He worshipped me; I worshipped him.

The years went by. Too fast, I think. We both got old. Our children grew up and went their separate ways on the road of life that leads to destiny. One day I looked at Ali and I saw his white hair. Somehow, his gait was not as quick. But his sweet smile was still the same. His eyes were still dark and deep. When I looked into his eyes, I still saw the stars; I still saw the sky. I saw the love he had for me.

The end came fast. The years went by too quickly. All things must end. I think of him and of our love. It was a love that only a few people on this earth get to experience. It was a love that began one summer in Egypt, one magic summer in Egypt, a magic summer that lasted seventy years. Seventy years that passed like the blink of an eye. My life does not mean anything to me now. I cannot live without him. I cannot live without my Ali. He meant the world to me; the strange world that he introduced me to became my own. I never really introduced him to my world. The summer of my seventeenth birthday was the last time that I saw Greece.

Xenia

Dear Journal,

Many years before I was introduced to my husband, I had a strange dream. In my dream, I saw a valley; I saw a field. I am not too sure. That detail evades me. There were partridges all around, those beautiful birds with their rich feathers and proud strut. There were partridges all around but one of them stood out. This one did not have feathers. But it stood out above the rest. I woke up in a cold sweat because I knew just what it meant. Years later, I married my American husband. My American husband who came to Greece to visit family. We were married two weeks after we were introduced. When he was getting my papers ready, I realized one thing. I realized that my husband was that partridge. He borrowed money for the two tickets to America. Dear journal, I do not know if he has paid them off. I do not ask.

For me it is so painful. All I know is that ever since the time of the Olympian gods, the Greeks knew how to interpret dreams. In rare cases where they could not, they would summon a high priest to interpret the dream for them. I knew what that dream meant. Life here is difficult. But I do not complain because I am in America. I work as a finisher in a factory and I am making money. I am making more money here than I ever imagined and more than I could ever make in Greece. Life here is difficult. But I have dreams. I have a dream that one day I, too, will be rich because America is the land of opportunity. I knew how to interpret that dream.

Maria

Dear Journal,

I married a man I do not love for he is not my equal. Forgive me for making such a statement but I just cannot help myself. Yes, he is kind to me and to the children but that is not enough for me. He is not the man of my dreams; he never was the man of my dreams. In Greece I loved another man. Our families knew each other on the island and then the two of us met. When we met, I felt that we were meant for each other. But we were not. He told me that he loved me and that he could not envision his life without me. But things happen. Everything changes. My father was a merchant. He had a ship that carried goods from one Greek island to the next. He made a lot of money. My future and that of his other daughters looked good. Life was good. But things happen. One day there were strong winds. His ship could not withstand the tumultuous seas. It sank. Our future sank because our father had invested much money in that ship. We lost our entire life savings. We were left destitute. I lost my marriage prospect. He told me he could not marry me. He told me that I should board the next ship to America. I was devastated. How could that be? How could he tell me just like that to board the next ship to America? I did. Oh, my dear journal, here I am. Here I am, married to a man I do not love.

When I came here, I did not know a soul. I got a job. I worked as a governess. I met people who introduced me to other people. I rejected marital possibilities. However, how long could that go on? I accepted my husband's proposal. We got married but I am miserable.

But something strange happened. I just want you to know that I have no one else really to talk to, just you, my dear journal. I want to tell you what happened. My husband and I went to Greece. We went back to my island. I had been gone a long time, a very long time. One night we decided to go for a walk. We walked along the shore by the beautiful Aegean Sea, to breathe the fresh air, to smell the sea, to enjoy life. I saw a taverna on the distant horizon. I saw silhouettes. I saw the silhouettes and one stood out. I recognized it right away. It could not be! It was my love! The love that I had left behind on the island many years ago when I boarded the ship, the ship that took me in its arms and cradled me, and brought me to the States. We had not seen each other for close to forty years. I did not want him to know I was unhappy. I wanted him to think I was in love. I wanted him to think that I was happy. I took my husband's hand in mine and held it. I kept holding it as we approached. He turned to look at us. He turned to look at me. I briefly filled him in. I left out many things. I did not tell him that I think of him. I did not tell him I cannot forget. What good would that do? He spoke with his lips; he spoke with his eyes. I knew. I knew that he could not forget. I knew he was unhappy. He turned to see my husband. He turned to see my husband and told him that he envies him. He envies him. That's all he said. Three little words that spoke so much.

Elena

Dear Journal,

I do not know just what to do. However, I do know what to expect. I am the youngest of the four. I am the youngest girl. My mother's first child was a boy. It is a heavy cross to bear when you are an only son among three girls. The Greeks demand. They demand of their sons if they have female siblings. My brother was told what to do. He has to work, make money, and send it to the village for our dowries. Without dowries, we cannot marry. Who will marry us if we do not have money or a house? But just how much can he do? Just how much can he work? I do not know. The future scares me, my dear journal. My two older sisters work in the fields. They get up at the crack of dawn and go out to the fields to pick the olives. They carry rods with which they shake the olive trees and the olives drop in the baskets that they have put on the ground under the tree. Sometimes, they climb on ladders and shake the branches from up there. It is very hard work. They are there under the noonday sun and they are there until the sun sets on the horizon. I am afraid. When I reach my sixteenth birthday, they will take me out of school. They will take me out of school to work in the olive fields. Two days ago, we got a letter from our brother. He wrote my father that he wants to be a writer. He wants to be a poet. He wants to sit at the Parisian cafes, he said, and do just what he wants. How can that be? What will become of us? Who will send us the money for our dowries? Who will send us a ticket out of this hard life? Oh, my dear journal, I'm so afraid. I am afraid because I know. The future scares me, my dear journal, because I know what to expect. It is still dark outside as I am writing this. My sisters have just gotten up. I am afraid because I know.

Eleftheria

Dear Journal,

Perhaps it seems strange to you that I am writing a journal entry. Why? Is that just meant for women? Are men not allowed to jot down their feelings and their thoughts? If they are not, then let me break from custom. I am the eldest child. I am the eldest child of five. The other four are girls. Yes, girls. Do you know what that means? It means that I should be their supporter and provider. The family has exiled me. Yes, they exiled me. My father gave me a ticket to Brazil and told me to work, send money, and marry off my sisters. How can I work so much? What about me? Do I not count? And how much should I send for each? Well, that depends, they said. That depends on the future husband of each of my sisters when the time comes and he should be found. He can ask for as much money as he wants. Yes, that's right, for as much money as he wants. My eldest sister of the four was fixed up with a man who was extremely poor. But it was a marriage prospect, our father said. He picked olives in the fields. He worked from dawn to dusk. He asked for enough money to buy a home in town. I worked two jobs to make ends meet. I sent the money for the house. He married her. But that was not enough. Six months after the wedding, my father sent me a letter. In it he stated that my sister's husband asked for more money. He said that her husband told them his brother got much more from the woman he was about to marry. My sister's husband felt cheated. If he did not get what he was asking for, my father wrote, he would divorce my sister. Yes, that's right. He would divorce her. How much more did he want? How much more can you send? That was their reply. I worked two jobs to make ends meet. I sent them enough money to add another room to their house. And then there were the other three. The three remaining sisters. At this rate, I would never put anything aside for me. I would never have enough money to start a family of my own. My father wrote me a letter. In it he wrote that I was not to return to the island until I had married off all my remaining sisters. How long would that take? I did not know. I got confused; I got depressed. I thought about a lot of things. I weighed the pros and cons. Did anybody care for me? I do not know. My father sent me letters. He asked what was taking me so long and why I was not sending any money. Why I did not respond. He never asked about my health. They never heard from me again. I never sent another note. I do not know what became of my sisters. I do not know what became of my parents. They never heard from me again. In my dreams I see my beautiful island with the orange trees. I smell the eucalyptus and the hyacinth. I see the bougainvillaeas in full bloom, their blossoms hanging over the white-washed walls of the neoclassical houses whose arched doors are painted blue or green or brown. I see the tiles on the roofs as they glisten from the raindrops that resemble my tears. I see the golden rays of the sun spread over the blue-green sea and I hear the waves rolling back and forth, back and forth, hitting against the fishing boats and the caiques in the harbor. Both my children speak Portuguese. They want to see the island. They want to visit the island of their ancestors. They want to take me with them. Perhaps one day....

Yiorgos

Chapter Twenty-Two

Greeks Making Headlines

Young Girl Kidnapped While Gathering Flowers

Persephone Ceresopoulos, 18, was abducted early this morning while gathering flowers in the Athenian Valley. The alleged perpetrator who, according to witnesses, resembles the victim's uncle, swung the victim into his chariot, whipped the four black horses, and sped off towards an undisclosed location.

Demeter Ceresopoulos, 38, distraught as she spoke to reporters, pleaded with the kidnapper for the safe return of her daughter. She stated that she is willing to go to the ends of the Earth to retrieve her and is ready to make any deals necessary. The police have no clues regarding the motive.

Top Musician's Wife Poisoned by Snake

Eurydice, wife of renowned lyricist and master poet Orpheus, expired early this morning after being bitten by a poisonous snake while walking along the banks of the Hebrus River in the company of the river nymphs.

Orpheus has consulted with a liaison who maintains contact between this world and the next. After participating in a seance, Orpheus emphatically states he was literally transported to the Underworld where he bargained with Hades, the grim keeper of Everything Beneath the Earth, for the release of Eurydice. Orpheus has not upheld the condition which states that he should not look back on his way out, forcing Eurydice to return from whence she came. He has gone into a deep clinical depression and has been admitted to Bellevue for psychological observation.

First Woman in the History of Ancient Greece to Conceive by In-Vitro

Hera, wife of Zeus, the top man of Olympus Consultants, has recently given birth to a baby boy conceived by in-vitro in her attempt to avenge her philandering husband. Hera refuses to explain how she availed herself of all the medical knowledge required to successfully bring such a procedure to fruition. It is suspected that she sought the assistance of the great healer and god of all medicine, Aesculapius. In honor of the secret code of medicine, the details regarding the donor cannot be disclosed. Hence, the identity of the father of Hephaestus will remain a secret unto all eternity.

Coastal Sea and Island Finally Named

Icarus, a renowned architect in his own right and son of the famous architect Daedalus, drowned after plunging into the sea early this morning while father and son attempted to escape from the island of Crete where they were being held hostage by the Cretan king, Minos. Upon realizing his plight, the victim called for help at the top of his lungs. His distraught father made a futile attempt to catch him. High tides made it impossible for rescuers to approach. Witnesses state that Icarus was flying an erratic path too near the sun causing the wax holding the feathers together on his wings to melt. A rescue team has since been dispatched to retrieve the body. The locals have voted to name that immediate body of water that blends with the Aegean the "Icarian Sea" and the nearest island "Icaria" as a sign of tribute.

An A-Maze-ing Feat (Day One)

Theseus, Prince of Athens and son of the ruling King Aegeus, has arrived in Crete where he will attempt to slay the Minotaur. He was met by the King's daughter Ariadne who, it is reported, has fallen madly in love with him. Distraught at the thought that Theseus may not be able to find his way out of the maze should he slay the beast, Ariadne has supplied him with a ball of thread, instructing him to unwind it upon entering and following it out once again to the exit. Meanwhile, Aegeus in Athens nervously awaits the sight of his son's ship on the horizon.

An A-Maze-ing Feat (Day Two)

Theseus, Prince of Athens and son of the ruling King Aegeus, has slain the monster in the labyrinth in Knossos thus freeing his city of the punishment mandating the city-state of Athens to send twelve of its youth every year for the Minotaur to devour. As per the directions of the King's daughter Ariadne, Theseus retraced his steps to the exit of the maze by rewinding the ball of thread he unwound as he entered. It is reported that Ariadne, swearing eternal love for Theseus, has fled the island with him infuriating King Minos who has vowed revenge. The happy couple plan to make Athens their home where it is expected that Ariadne will be welcomed by Aegeus with open arms.

An A-Maze-ing Feat (Day Three)

Ariadne, daughter of King Minos of Crete, reportedly has been deserted by Theseus on the island of Naxos on their way back to Athens after Theseus successfully slew the Minotaur and found his way out of the maze with her assistance. Hours prior to her being deserted, Theseus was seen consulting with Bacchus, god of wine and mirth. It is strongly suspected that the Prince of Athens was following the deity's orders. No further information is available at the present time.

SEA-soned Events (Day Four)

King Aegeus of the city-state of Athens has drowned after jumping into the sea early this morning. Having instructed Theseus to change the sails from black to white on his return trip from Crete should he be successful in slaying the monster, Aegeus became distraught at the sight of the black sails and at the thought that his beloved son had been devoured by the Minotaur. As a sign of respect and love for their King, the Athenians have cast their votes to give the sea around the city-state of Athens his name. Hence, from this day forward, that body of water shall be known as the Aegean Sea.

Wedding Date Set for Theseus

It has been announced throughout the land that Theseus, King of the city-state of Athens, will enter the bonds of marriage with his beloved Hyppolyte, Queen of the Amazons, on the day when the sun shines on the land for a period of twelve hours without interruption. Preparations are under way for the nuptials that will begin at dawn and end at midnight. It has been reported that Theseus has never been happier and that he plans to make his beloved equally happy. Let this reporter remind the plebeians of the city-state of Athens that this is the same Theseus who slew the Minotaur on the island of Crete thus freeing his people from the Cretan curse. This is the same Theseus who deserted Ariadne, his benefactor, on the Cycladic island of Naxos. This is the same Theseus who partied so much on the ship that he forgot to change the sails from black to white resulting in his father's suicide. All that put aside, let us wish the happy couple much good luck and a life of eternal bliss together.

Royal Child Abuse

Hera, wife of unfaithful Zeus and goddess of marriage and family, has thrown her toddler Hephaestus off the summit of Mount Olympus in a fit of desperation and anger. Hephaestus brought his mother to the point of infanticide after continuously disobeying her commands for many months on end. Witnessing the fall, the neighboring shepherds claim the toddler hit the earth after three whole days. He has been taken to their hut where he was offered warm blankets and nourishment. Upon medical examination by skilled healers of Lesvos, it was observed that the victim injured his leg on impact. The prognosis is such that Hephaestus will sustain a limp for the duration of eternity.

Happily Ever After?

Hephaestus, god of fire and metal, and Aphrodite, goddess of love and beauty, have announced their nuptials as they have been so ordained by the gods and goddesses of Mount Olympus. Hephaestus, upon hearing that he was fated to wed the most beautiful of all goddesses and of all mortal women, jumped for joy to the best of his ability. He has sustained a limp after being thrown off Mount Olympus years ago by his distraught and angry mother Hera. Aphrodite, upon hearing she was fated to wed the ugliest of all gods and of all mortal men, fainted in the arms of the sea nymphs. Aphrodite has since vowed to be unfaithful to her husband. This has caused much concern in the world of the immortals and in the world of the mortals as well, whereupon the reporters have decided to follow the marriage carefully and to produce forth a case study for evaluation and analysis.

Net Gain

Hephaestus, god of fire and metal, was mortified at the sight of his wife Aphrodite, goddess of love and beauty, in the arms of her lover Ares, god of war, early this morning. The two were netted in by an undetectable-to-the-eye net that gave way at their slightest touch. The net was placed over their bed by the cuckolded husband after he was informed of his wife's infidelity by the Great Sun that sees and hears it all. Hephaestus has summoned the gods and goddesses of Mount Olympus to be witness to the spectacle, much to the bewilderment of the two disgraced lovers. The incident has caused much laughter and merriment among the deities. It is speculated that the gods of Mount Olympus envy Ares and wish they could have been in his place.

Chapter Twenty-Three

Traditions

I was born the daughter of a rich merchant on the island. My father was the heir to twenty-two shops and six-hundred-seventy-five heads of livestock. Each of his shops featured items such as crystal bowls and vases, porcelain cups and saucers, bronze and copper candlestick holders, and silver tea sets with the heavy silver tray to match. Each tray, I remember distinctly, had silver designs embossed all around on the border, with a matching design on the handles. Of what significance is all that now? Things come to mind. No matter how many years go by, some things stay with you and become part of you. The gold currency flowed in like the water flows in a river, in a brook, from a cataract. For my dowry alone, Father planned to give me two of his shops; two of his shops that brought in enough money every month for me to buy more property, more houses.

I grew up when the island was under the Turkish occupation. We could not go to school; no Greek subjects were taught in any institution. Father wanted me to learn to read and write in Greek so that I should maintain our language and our heritage. He was adamant. This was very important to him. He hired the best tutors. I was taught Greek at home. I was taught ancient Greek, French, German, and Latin. I became fluent in all languages. My brothers were taught how to keep the books and how to do business with our customers. Our shops were frequented by Turks. Yes, the same Turks who denied us our rights, our language, our religion, and our traditions. Business on the island was carried on as usual because the Turkish magistrate had made an agreement that some of the merchandise would be offered to the pasha as a gift. That included wool, leather goods, silver, fruits and nuts. In exchange, our island would be more or less left alone and sometimes would not have to pay the magistrate the taxes imposed on other islands and regions. At one point, things were so confusing for everybody because there was a lack of communication between the pasha, the oppressors, and the islanders.

We lived in an exclusive part of town. Our neighbors were all just as rich, if not richer, and their children were also taught by the best. We all had servants. Servants who cleaned, who cooked, who took care of everything that needed to be done in the house so that we would not have to do anything except spend the day at leisure. Our house was a fifteen-room mansion. It was given to Mother as a dowry when she was about to marry Father. The wood for the banisters and the marble for the tiles on the floors had been imported from Italy. Mother's father had hired the best carpenters and masons to do the work. Two rooms on the western end of our mansion had been set aside as servants' quarters.

Father's livestock was overseen by ranchers whom he paid very well. The sheep and cattle grazed in the fields on the outskirts of town. Before the occupation, my grandfather sold the wool that was made into the finest material to the neighboring countries and, yes, it even went as far as the Russian ports. Odessa was brimming with Greeks. When the Turks invaded the island, things changed. It was virtually impossible to ship the merchandise to other ports but Father managed to do so. On occasion, there were raids. The Turks slaughtered the livestock just for the fun of it, the same way they slaughtered people. The horses galloped into coffee shops at full speed while their riders overturned tables, chairs, and anything else in their paths. Dishes, cups, and saucers ended up on the floor. They did this in an attempt to instill morbid fear in the shop owners and their customers. No one dared venture to the mountains either alone or even in groups because that is where the Turks were hiding. They waited for the "Rayiah", the Turkish derogatory term for the Greeks, and emerged on horseback, their swords extended, in pursuit of their victims. The Turks skinned the Greeks alive. They were skinned on the spot, their skin made into tobacco pouches for the pashas and the sultans in the harems on the larger Greek islands and in some towns. That was their punishment; their punishment for being Greek. There was talk on the island that in the villages the Greeks were killed mercilessly. The merchants who had won the favor of the Turks by offering of their goods had access to the forbidden Turkish houses of pleasure. They were allowed to enter to conduct their business. There, on the low tables, they would notice a "nargileh" or peace pipe, and a tobacco pouch right next to it. A tobacco pouch that had been made from the skin of a Greek.

There was talk that on the island of Crete the Cretan warriors would take on the Turks two and three at a time. Descendants of the Dorians, the Cretans were fearless. The Turks did not make themselves too obvious on the island because they knew. They knew that they had met their match and then some. There was more talk. The inhabitants of smaller islands hid in the fortresses and waited. In their midst, they had pots and pans full of hot oil that they poured on the Turks as they ascended the slopes. This was their defense. They had no other weapons; they had no other recourse. As a young girl, I listened carefully to all the details. I admired these warriors.

Father simply could not forget the day in our history, he kept saying, when Constantinople, that beautiful city near the Bosporus named for Constantine the Great when he moved the capital of the Roman Empire from the West to the East in 323 A.D., fell to the Turks. He remembered the night his father came home and told the family the terrible news. He remembered that night, Tuesday, May 29, 1453, as if it were yesterday. After that, the Turks were able to invade Greece and establish their presence with little trouble. Father just could not understand why.

I was afraid to leave the house. I didn't know what to expect. Anyway, Father would not allow it. He said I was too beautiful. Too beautiful for my own good. I felt asphyxiated. I could not breathe in my own home.

The years went by. He wanted to marry me off to the son of another opulent merchant. He made the deals. He made the deals and said that for my dowry he would write my name on two deeds to two shops. Then there was more talk. He would make more deals. He would make a deal with the ship captains to smuggle my future husband and me out of the island, out of the country, until this would be over. Would I go to the Russian ports? Would I go to Odessa? He said I would stay in Odessa until this would be over. Just until this would be over. How long would this occupation last? How long would we be slaves on our own soil? Who could give an accurate response? No one, really. But the more the enemy occupies a certain piece of land, I heard Father say, the stronger the enemy becomes. How much longer would it be?

One night, I saw an elderly gentleman sitting in our parlor. I did not ask who he was because it was not proper. I assumed that he was another merchant doing business with Father. The next day I was told that he was my future father-in-law, that I would be marrying his son. My heart skipped a beat. Marrying his son? How could that be?

I had never laid eyes on his son. I did not know what his son was like. I did not say a word. Father's word was law.

It was arranged for the priest to come to the house to perform the ceremony under lock and key. We could not go to our church. The open practice of religion was strictly forbidden. The details of my wedding were taken care of by Father and the servants. The wedding day was drawing near. I did not know what to expect. Would I remain on the island? Would I be forced to leave in the middle of the night? I did not know. I did not ask.

I distinctly remember what followed as if it were yesterday even though forty years have gone by. Forty years since then and we are still under the Turkish occupation. How many more years will go by while we remain under the Turkish yoke? I do not know. I do not ask. No one really knows. All I know is that things did not go as planned. I remember this as if it were yesterday. How can I possibly forget? It was a warm, balmy night. There was a full moon in the sky. I know because I stood out on our balcony and looked up at the sky. The sky that was full of stars that night, the stars that looked down on our miserable little world and knew how unhappy we were. The stars that served as witnesses to that which was to come.

The next night, I was kidnapped by the pasha's faithful servant. He was sent to kidnap me after the pasha saw me standing on our balcony. I did not see the pasha or his horse that night. I did not hear the horse neigh, if it did. I do not remember because that part now is a blur. All I know is that on the night before my wedding, the Turkish waif entered my room. He climbed the date tree, swung onto the balcony leading into my bedroom, held his hand over my mouth, and ordered me not to make a sound. He said if I did, he would slit my throat. I froze. I tried to scream but I could not. At that moment, I really did not care had he done so. I tried to free myself but I could not. He dragged me out onto the balcony and from there pushed me to one of his men who, with one leg on horseback and one leg on our date tree, grabbed me with both arms, held me tightly and whipped his horse that took off at lightning speed. I thought that it was all a dream; I thought that it was all a nightmare. I thought I would wake up and find myself in my warm bed with the canopy above me, in my bed covered with the bedspread that Father had bought for me from Constantinople many years before. I thought that I would wake up and find myself in my warm bed on my mattress, the mattress stuffed with goose feathers, the kind of mattress only the rich possessed.

I was dragged into the harem. I did not know on which island. I did not know in which village. I did not ask. I was just dazed. This could not be happening to me. I looked into the pasha's eyes. I looked into his eyes and my hair stood on end. I looked into his eyes and my blood ran cold. I looked into his eyes and wanted to throw up. He made me his that night.

Father was furious. How could such shame befall the family? How could the pasha do this to him? How could the pasha do this to his daughter? Did he not give the pasha enough silver? Did he not give the pasha enough of what he asked? Father made deals. He wanted me back at all costs. The pasha claimed he was in love with me and would not hear of it. I was caught in the middle. At that point, it did not matter anymore. It did not matter because my life was ruined. My life was ruined the night I was kidnapped by the pasha's faithful servant. Of course, the marriage prospect was off. No amount of money could erase the shame that went with the kidnapping. No amount of money could restore my chastity. I never got to meet the boy who would have become my husband. To this day, forty years after the incident, I think about him. I create him in my mind. I create him in my heart. But he remains a mystery.

The pasha's faithful servant brought me home. I would not look my father in the eye. I was ashamed. Mother did not say a word. But I knew what she felt. She was ashamed. She was ashamed, yet she also felt sorry for me. Sorry for her rich, beautiful, privileged daughter who was not worth a thing.

I locked myself in my room. That same room that served as a stepping stone to my catastrophe. The years went by. Mother wanted me to have somebody in my life for when the time came and my parents were no longer here. But who would have me? Who would have spoiled merchandise and soiled by a Turk, no less? We had servants. Servants who cleaned, who cooked, who took care of everything that needed to be done in the house so that we would not have to do anything except spend the day at leisure. Years after I was abducted, I married one of those servants. One of those servants who did not have a penny to his name except the roof above his head that my father's house provided. Right before he married me, he requested that our house be turned over to him. Our house, my mother's house, Mother's dowry, was given to him. A day before my wedding, my father went up to the attic, opened the trunk in which all the important papers were kept, took out the piece of paper his father-in-law had given him a day before his wedding, and wrote the servant's name on the deed. He wrote the servant's name on the deed because the servant was the only man who was willing to marry his daughter, my father's daughter, the daughter who had brought shame to the family.

Chapter Twenty-Four

More Greek Traditions

America continued to witness a tremendous influx of Greeks well into the nineteen fifties and nineteen sixties. The Greeks packed their clothes and hopes in trunks and crossed the Atlantic in steamships. During these two decades, the "Olympia" and "Queen Frederica" transported the Greeks from Piraeus, docking on 42nd Street and 12th Avenue, after stopping in Naples, Rome, and Halifax. The Italian "Vulcania" and "Saturnia" sailed from Patras. The Rex Hotel in New York served as a home for the Greeks in transit to other destinations.

The first thing the Greeks did and still do in their new communities is build a church, a spiritual bastion. That is where they congregate on Sundays to pray and where their weddings, baptismals, and funerals take place. That is where they socialize during the coffee hour. Many churches also house Greek schools.

In Manhattan alone, including Spanish Harlem and Washington Heights, they built churches and more churches, all in close proximity to each other. The church of St. George has a special place in my heart. That is where I was baptized. As a child, I was always awed whenever I glanced at the icon on the church wall depicting St. George on horseback slaying the dragon. The church of the Archangel Michael was located near my apartment in the Garment District and that is the church we frequented most often. The church of St. Eleftherios, patron saint of the enslaved and the downtrodden, is situated a few blocks away. Expectant mothers pray to this saint in hopes of a safe delivery. The church of St. John the Baptist is not far from there.

When the Greeks made money, they moved to Astoria. It was affordable and conveniently located right over the 59th Street Bridge. The houses were ideal because they had gardens and back yards. A garage was not a necessity; it was an amenity.

In Astoria alone, there are six Greek churches, some on the old calendar. To a Greek, Easter is the holiest holiday and the only one the old and new calendarists celebrate together. It is a resurrection. On Good Friday, the service is something special. The "Epitaphios", a make-shift tomb of Christ with an icon in its center, is adorned with carnations and lilies of the valley. Four men carry the Epitaphios on their shoulders accompanied by the priest and the parishioners as they all solemnly proceed around the neighborhood while a band plays dirges. This is a re-enactment of Christ's funeral. On that day, even the most gluttonous Greek fasts as a sign of respect. The processions of Saint Catherine, Saint Markella and Saint Irene Chrysovalantou meet at a designated crosspoint at a certain time. It has become a ritual. We carry lit candles and we boast that our Epitaphios is the prettiest.

On Holy Saturday night we must bring home the Holy Light for good luck. At midnight, the priest turns off the lights in the church to replicate Christ's tomb. We can hear a pin drop and this is one of the rare times the Greeks are absolutely quiet. Emerging from the sanctuary with a lit candle in his hand, the priest passes the Holy Light from his candle to ours. We chant "Christ is Risen from the dead giving us eternal life" and we exit the church to chant outside. The sound of firecrackers deafens the crowd. We are given a red egg for good luck and if a candle blows out we rekindle it from the candles of the parishioners around us. I carry the Holy Light in a lantern my cousin in Symi made for me.

We go home to enjoy a feast consisting of "magiritsa", a soup usually made of lamb's intestines, kidneys and hearts. We call it "gut soup". This is washed down with retsina, a Greek resin wine. We crack red eggs with one another as a sign of the victory of life over death and if our egg shell does not crack, we will be lucky all year.

At the crack of dawn on Easter Sunday, the Greeks prepare the "arni", the lamb for the skewer, or "souvla". It is roasted for hours over a pit. They take turns at the handle while Greek music blasts the neighborhood. A Greek roasts the lamb even if it means setting up the equipment in front of his garage near the sidewalk. On Easter Sunday of 2003, on the way to the home of my cousins in Bayside, we witnessed such a sight on a street in Astoria. If you didn't know the ethnicity of your neighbors, you find out on Greek Easter.

When the lamb is finally roasted, we sit down to a dinner fit for a king. We crack eggs with one another. It is tradition. We eat more magiritsa. The main meal consists of roasted lamb, lemon potatoes, and rice. Only a Greek will serve both lemon potatoes and rice in place of vegetables. Of course, there is always a Greek salad. And retsina. Who can forget retsina? It is the national wine of Greece. Dessert follows. The "tsoureki", or Easter bread, is a must. Baklava, kataif, galaktoboureko (fillo dough filled with custard), and koulourakia adorn the table. Everybody has a little of everything. The next day we all worry about our cholesterol. Actually, a Greek doesn't worry much. To him, life is like a fairy tale.

Astoria's demographics have changed. Many Greeks have moved to other neighborhoods such as Bayside and Long Island because they made more money. No matter where a Greek migrates, he will roast the lamb in his front yard, in his back yard, or on the sidewalk because tradition is tradition.

Chapter Twenty-Five

Roots

When Smyrna fell to the Turks in 1922, I was a child of twelve. It has been many years but I cannot forget. The fires burned for days. The sky, usually blue, the same shade of blue as the stripes on the Greek flag, became black. The smoke covered the clouds, the sky, the atmosphere.

I was born in Smyrna. I knew no other land. To me, Smyrna had been my home until that fateful day. Our house was situated by the shore, by the sea, by the same sea that blends with the sea of Greece, the home of my ancestors. It was a beautiful house that my parents built when I was born being that my father's business had been doing well. My father was a tanner. He worked with leather and he worked with hides. He made a lot of money. His family had relocated to Smyrna from the island. I remember my father saying that his father and his father's father were from Chios. During the time of the Turkish occupation of Greece, Chios was exempt from paying taxes to the Turks because of its mastic trees. That soft, sap-like substance was manufactured into gum. It was the mastic from the mastic trees that kept the sultan happy, happy enough so as to overlook the stringent laws other parts of subjugated Greece were struggling to deal with. My mother was from Polis. My parents met when my father went to Constantinople to deliver some merchandise. He fell madly in love with her. He brought my mother from her native city to his.

My father's brother owned vineyards. I remember the luscious grapes of green and black growing on the vines, clinging to the trellises that Uncle had built in the fields. Similar grapes were always hanging over the walls of the

103

houses in the alleys. I remember the camels, the camels that transported all that delicious fruit to market. They would pass by our house. They would pass by our house and I would see the packs on their backs. I would see the grapes and the plums and the dates. I tried to reach the fruit. I tried to reach but I could not. Mother always said we could have all the grapes we wanted from Uncle's vineyards. She said we could buy all the plums and dates we wanted from the market. She said we could have anything our little hearts desired.

I had just come home from school on that fateful day that marks the holocaust of the Greeks. Mother said we had to leave quickly. I was not to ask questions. I wanted to know why. We hastily packed our things. What could I take with me? What did I know? I relied on Mother to take for me what she thought I would need. I did not see my father as I usually did when I came home from school. I did not see Grandfather or Uncle. Grandmother was crying. Mother told me that the men had been rounded up and taken somewhere to be interrogated. She said that they would all be back in time to meet us at the harbor. The harbor? What exactly was happening? Where exactly were we going?

When I stepped outside, I could not breathe. The black smoke filled my childish lungs and I began to cough. Mother gave me a white handkerchief with which to cover my nose and mouth. I did as I was told. My eyes searched the crowd. The crowd that was passing by before us, the crowd that was headed for the boats, the crowd that consisted only of women and children. Where were all the men? I looked for my father. I looked for Uncle and for Grandfather. Then I began to cry. I did not want to leave. I did not want to leave without my father. My mother grabbed my arm. She dragged me all the way to the harbor, all the way to the harbor where the boats were waiting for us, waiting to take us far away from there, waiting to take us to some unknown land. We heard the gun shots on the distant horizon. The gunshots that went on non-stop for what seemed an eternity. Mother started to cry. And so did Grandmother. And I cried without knowing why.

Too many packs. That's what he said. Too many packs. You could not carry two bundles aboard. "Don't you *understand*?", he shouted at her. "They take up too much room. Drop one, otherwise you do not get in." What could she do? She seemed confused and anxious. Afraid that she would be left out, she nervously dropped one bundle into the sea. I was eyeing all this very carefully. How many bundles did we have? Before I could even finish my train of thought, I heard a shrill that penetrated my ears, my brain, my entire being. I was a child but to this day I cannot forget. Distraught upon realizing what she had done, she jumped into the sea after it as in an effort to retrieve her bundle, to retrieve her error, to retrieve her infant, the infant she had dropped mistakenly into the sea.

I grabbed my mother's hand. I felt so lost. We climbed into the boat and sat on the floor. I was squashed but I did not say a word; I did not make a sound. I could not move. I could not see the horizon, the sea, or the sky. The black smoke continued to rise, to cover the clouds, to pollute the air, to travel across the sky. It seemed so macabre and so unreal. My beloved Smyrna was burning to the ground.

The women around us would not stop crying. They would not stop wailing. It seemed to me as if they were calling out names. An older woman sitting across from us was pulling her hair and slapping her face. She told my mother they had taken her husband and three sons. Her husband and three sons. They did not take their wives. The Turks had taken all the men but left the women to fend for themselves. And what about the children? Who would care for the children?

When we reached Mytilene it was already midnight. I could not see a thing. Some people met us at the harbor. We were taken to their house for the night. The next morning, my mother woke me very early. So early, in fact, that it was still dark. There were things to do and papers to get. The struggle for survival had begun.

Too many years have gone by. Too many years but I do not forget. I am now a grown man with a business and a family of my own. I talk to my children of the life I had in Smyrna. I tell my children of their grandfather's tanning business and of their grandmother's relocating from Polis to Smyrna, to Mytilene. They listen to me and do not make a sound. I tell my children of their great-uncle's vineyards. Sometimes I go to market. I need to keep busy. I go to market to forget and to remember. I see the grapes on the stands. The luscious grapes of green and black that grew on the vines in Uncle's vineyards, the grapes that grew on the vines hanging over the walls of the houses in the alleys. I remember the camels. The camels that transported all that delicious fruit to market. They would pass by our house. They would pass by our house and I would see the packs on their backs. I would see the grapes and the plums and the dates. I try to reach the fruit. I try to reach but I cannot. Mother used to say we could have all the grapes from Uncle's vineyards and we could buy all the plums and dates we wanted from the market. She used to say that we could have everything our little hearts desired. It is one of life's ironies that we can have everything our little hearts desire, everything that our money can buy, but we cannot have what our little hearts truly, truly desire. We cannot have our heritage; we cannot have our roots.

Chapter Twenty-Six

Reminiscing

It all seems like a dream to me now but here I am remembering the details that I will put down on this page. That voyage back to my roots, to the island of my ancestors, seems like a dream but it was real. The island of my roots is known as Symi. It is a little island in the Dodecanese, an hour and forty-five minutes by boat from the island of Rhodes. How many people know of it? It is so small and insignificant to some but not to me. To me, it is so big, in fact, and so important, I have to grow two hearts to fit it in.

Symi was visited by important personnages of the Trojan War. Yes, that is how old it is and more. All the Achaean kings visited Symi on their way back from Troy. It seems unreal but it is true. Symi's king, Nireus, sailed off to Troy with the kings of Rhodes and Kos. Just think, Nireus knew Achilles, the greatest of all warriors of the Trojan War. He knew Odysseus, the Sailor of all sailors. He knew the two brothers, King Agamemnon of Mycenae and King Menelaus of Sparta. Yes, *the* King Menelaus, husband of Helen. Ah, Helen, whose face it was that launched a thousand ships. Symi alone sent three triremes to Troy. However, Nireus did not return because it was not meant to be. His mother, AEgli, sat atop the majestic mountains of Symi and looked out on the horizon as she waited to see her son's trireme approach. At that time, the island had her name. At that time, the island was called AEgli.

According to legend, when the island was visited by Glafkos, it underwent a change. He was received warmly by the islanders. He was so pleased, he taught them a trade. He taught them a trade that would help them to earn their livelihood and to survive. He taught them how to caulk the ships. And that's not all. He gave the island of AEgli the name of his beloved wife, which happened to be Symi. And Symi has borne that name ever since.

Dear Symi, you are the island of my ancestors. That summer, that special summer, I felt your arms around me. I felt enveloped by my roots. I visited my yiayia's house. I walked inside her courtyard. I walked on the stone steps on which she and her mother and her mother's mother used to tread. Where are they now? Where are all these grandmothers? If these stone steps could talk, what would they say? What would they tell me? These stone steps lead to somewhere. They lead to the two bedrooms on the upper level of the house; they lead to the courtyard on the lower level of the house. They lead to my past; they lead to my future. I saw my yiayia's kitchen. It was so small, it was unreal. What did my yiayia cook in it? What did her mother cook in it? If these stone steps could talk, what would they tell me? They saw my yiayia cook. I know they did because they are right there. Right there, by my yiayia's kitchen in the courtyard of her house.

How could you know? How could you know, my yiayia, that one day, one day, a part of you, your daughter, my mother, would find herself thousands of miles away? Yiayia, it's called SURVIVAL. For you, my yiayia, it is a strange land. But not for us. For you, my yiayia, it is inhospitable. But not for us. We have scattered, my yiayia. We live in foreign countries and in foreign lands but I think of you often. I wrote you a poem about our sacred soil. In it I mention the grapevine, the grapevine you planted in our courtyard when you were pregnant with my mother. We are scattered all over, yiayia, we have branched out like the vine whose branches grew and blossomed but we have withered. Yiayia, we have withered because life took its toll.

Chapter Twenty-Seven

Double-Headed Eagle

I don't want any questions. Yes, I am a double-headed eagle. What does that mean? Well, let me tell you. It is the symbol of our faith. It is the symbol of the Greek existence, the Greek ethnicity, and the Greek faith. If you look at any formal papers of the Greek Archdiocese, you will see me on their official stamps. I represent orthodoxy; I represent the East and West. An eagle is a proud bird. Why is the eagle the official bird of the United States? You see, we represent freedom as well. The eagle is a majestic bird. It is the only bird that can fly so very high. Yes, when it rains the eagle flies above the clouds. That's right, above the clouds and near the sun. Do you know what the ancient Greeks used to say? A surgeon, yes, a surgeon, read on, has to have the heart of a lion, the eye of an eagle, the hand of a woman, and an education equal to none. You see? The eye of an eagle. Sharp, quick, and accurate. I have been everywhere and I have seen many things. No, I have not seen double of everything. But I have seen so many things and I have seen the details. Too many details, in fact. It does not matter how long exactly I've been around. Let's just say, I've been around. Come, let me tell you what I have seen. I may not be able to tell you everything, but I will try to give you a bird's eye view of history, Greek mythology, of anything I can. I may not tell you in order because I'm kind of old and I may not remember. But the details I do not forget. Come, fly with me.

I don't know what it is with me that I want to share this with you first. I can begin with something else, but I will not. Go back to 1941. Why 1941? Well, you will see. Go to Greece, May of 1941. I want to tell you what I saw. I flew over the Parthenon. It was a sorry sight. The enemy had draped its flag over that sacred building. It could be seen from the entire city of Athens, from every point, from everywhere one stood. And no one did dare say a word. But let me tell you what I saw. I witnessed something that was brave and that has made me proud. I do not know if you do know, but after I relate it, you will know. After you read this, you will see and you, too, if you are a Greek, you, too, will feel so proud. I saw the sentry as he walked. It was a long way from the Parthenon to where he had to go. But that is not the point. The point is that this enabled the two Greek boys to carry out their plan. Their plan was to bring down the flag of the enemy without getting caught. I saw all this. I flew above. They watched the sentry take his walk and reach the cut-off point. They saw him do an about-face and come up the path. He turned again. When he reached a certain point, the boys sprang into action. One of them kept watch. The other climbed up to bring down the enemy flag. One end got caught. They broke out into a cold sweat. It got tangled and he could not get it loose. Then the other boy climbed up. They got it loose just in time before the sentry came up the path once more. And when he did come up the path, and when he saw what had happened, don't ask me what. I flew away. The two Greek boys had run away and had managed to hide. The next day the entire city of Athens was abuzz. The Athenians awoke to a sight they could not believe. I flew close to the crowds to hear just what they said. I heard the names of the two boys. One was Manolis Glezos. The other one was named Apostolos Santas. What mothers gave birth to them? The two Greek boys had made me proud because acts like this show the world what it means to love your country and to fight for it. But then there was retaliation because acts like this infuriate the enemy when he realizes that he has been outwon.

I kept flying. Now I don't remember the order of things but I saw many things. I flew over Athens and I saw the Parthenon. It was during the Golden Age, when it was being built. Phidias oversaw the whole project. In case you don't know, Phidias was one of the best sculptors of ancient Greece. He made sure that Kallicrates and Iktinos, the architects of the Parthenon, carried out their plans as they had set out to do. And look, look at the temple that was built in honor of the goddess that gave the city-state its name! It has been so long, so many years have gone by, and here it still stands even though during the Turkish occupation it had its problems, too. The Turks built a minaret right smack in the center of the temple. Yes, that's right. They built a minaret. Why? I think to make it a place of worship for themselves. They also blew it up. That's right. They fired their cannon balls and blew it up. Well, despite the damage it sustained, it still stands. Yes, it does. It stands as a symbol of the Golden Age of Greece and as a symbol of the civilization of the land that gave the world so much. Let's move on.

Now, I'm getting confused. I am not sure if this happened before, during, or after the building of the Parthenon. The Olympian gods were ruling on Olympus. Come with me. As I flew over the earth I saw the sun god terribly annoyed. He was angry, in fact. He was in love. Oh, not again. He always fell in love. This time, it was with a maiden. Yes, a maiden. That's nice. Once before, he fell in love with a young lad but the lad did not reciprocate his love. So they say. At least, not the way the sun god wanted the lad to love him. They had gone in the woods to frolic and to hunt. Apollo threw his discus. It flew so high it almost hit me as I was flying by. Hyacinthus, the lad who was hunting with him, ran to participate in the games but did not wait until the discus had come down. Well, it hit him in the face and knocked the life right out of him. Apollo was distraught. He ran to him but to no avail. To make a long story short, the sun god decided to pay tribute to the lad. A flower sprang where his blood dropped. This flower was named after him; this flower has a deep red hue, something like violet, and its name is, yes, hyacinth. So let's get back to this other love of his. Let me tell you what happened. I saw it all. That's how I know. It seems the sun god was in love with a maiden whose father was a Persian king. Her name was Leucothoe. Well, the sun god had many women who were in love with him and one of these women was Clytie. She could not tolerate Apollo's loving Leucothoe, especially after she found out that the two had consummated their love. What do you think she did? Like a typical woman, she went to the king and told him of his daughter's love affair. The king was furious because his daughter had brought shame to the family. He sought her out and punished her. He buried her deep in the earth. He placed a heavy weight on top to make sure that she would be asphyxiated with no hopes of being rescued. When the sun god found out, he was so angry! He hated Clytie. See what she did? She tattled on their love, the king killed Leucothoe, Apollo was angry, and Clytie lost her love anyway. Well, he was never her love to begin with, but hey, now she really did not stand a chance. I saw her pine away. As I flew above, I saw her standing in the middle of the field, in the forest, on the road, looking up at the sky. It seems she kept her eye on him. She kept her eye on the god she loved but could not ever have. Then I saw something strange. Her countenance began to change. It seems she could not move. Her feet took root. And pretty soon, she was changed into, guess what? A flower! Yes, that's right. A flower. There she stands, looking up at the sky all day, following the sun god and his chariot, swaying, rotating all day long, looking at her love. It is a sad story but, hey, what can you do? Things happen. Sometimes I see her standing there, rooted to the earth, looking up at the sky.

One day I found myself in a forest. There was an oak. It had magical powers. How do I know? Let me tell you. I saw a maiden on the grass. I heard her mumble-jumble. I knew exactly what that was. She was making predictions. Obviously, she had fasted for three days after bathing and washing her hair in the sacred pond. I saw her as she lay on the grass. She looked up at the oak, went into a trance as she chewed on bay leaves, and received its messages. Strange! I strongly believe that nature has the power to communicate. I strongly believe that the trees have a heart, a soul, a mouth. She received its messages and was able to translate everything. Which reminds me of Pythia. She, too, was a medium. One of the best in ancient Greece. Sitting on her three-legged stool, she was able to predict the outcome of battles and of destiny. She could destroy nations and bring down kingdoms. She, too, bathed in the sacred pond and chewed on bay leaves. I have seen her in action. Countless pilgrims visited her shrine and all her predictions came to pass.

Speaking of bay leaves. Apollo, here we are again, fell in love with another maiden by the name of Daphne. By the way, the word daphne in Greek means bay leaf. Well, she was not in love with him. You know how things go. You can't always win in love. But the sun god was persistent. He chased her in the woodlands; he chased her in the groves. But she evaded him. She prayed to her father Peneus, the river, yes, the river, she prayed to him to let her be. He always pressured her to wed. Right then and there, with Apollo in pursuit, Daphne was given powers. Right in front of the sun god, and I saw all this, Daphne began to change and she became a laurel tree. I always see a laurel tree growing right by a river. I can tell you what else I know. All this happened because of Cupid. That's right. Vengeful, spiteful Cupid. He didn't really like Apollo because of his conceited attitude. I heard Cupid talk to himself, saying that he would take care of that. I saw him fly from Parnassus and come down to the forest. I saw him reach into his quiver and shoot a golden arrow into Apollo's heart. But when it came to Daphne, well, he did not do the same. In her heart he shot a blunt, dull, lead arrow which drove all love away. And Daphne could not help herself; and Daphne had no choice.

Women did not care too much for Apollo despite his being handsome. I think that bothered him. That's probably why he fell in love with so many women. I think he needed to prove something to himself. Do you know who Coronis is? Apollo fell in love with her. But she went off and married someone else while pregnant with Apollo's offspring. Well, Apollo was absolutely furious. Do you know what he did? He killed her. He killed Coronis, but managed to save the baby. Don't ask me how he did it. And it's a good thing he did because that baby was none other than Aesculapius. Yes, Aesculapius, the god of medicine who was able to resuscitate the dead. You see, Apollo designated the centaur Chiron to be his teacher. Chiron taught him many things, among them medicine. First quality medicine. He was able to bring the dead back to life, much to the chagrin of Pluto whose kingdom was empty. Pluto went to Zeus to complain. He in turn threw a thunderbolt at the good doctor and knocked him dead. But not before the doctor had heirs. Aesculapius had five children. He had three daughters and two sons. One of his daughters was Hygeia, the goddess of health. Hygeia was very beautiful. You can see a bust of the goddess in doctors' offices. Oh, and one more thing about Apollo. At the exact moment Apollo was born, two eagles flew off the summit of Mount Olympus in opposite directions. Zeus decreed that when the eagles criss-crossed, he would designate the point where they met the center of the earth. Years later, that was where Apollo's oracle was built--the oracle at Delphi.

I saw strange things in ancient Greece. One day as I was flying, I saw a ritual in honor of the goddess Artemis, twin sister of Apollo. This ritual is called Vravronia. It's a real Greek word, wouldn't you say? This ritual took place every five years because I remembered having seen this again five years before and again five years before that. Anyway, here is what was happening. Little girls were brought there as priestesses where they remained with the older priestesses until it was time for them to wed. They stayed in rooms that were around there, too. On the day of the celebration, the little girls, in yellow robes, did a strange dance and were called little bears. I heard the incantations. But I saw something that has made me wonder to this day. I saw a big piece of marble with marble columns on it all around. There was an incense burner on a marble table. I flew around and do you know what I saw? I saw the tomb of Iphigeneia. Yes, that's right. The Iphigeneia who was sacrificed at the altar so the gods should send a favorable wind allowing the Greek ships to set sail for Troy. She was rescued by Artemis. When you are a bird, you get to see a lot of things. You get to see things that a human being may never get to see. I saw the same ritual performed in Athens. When the women were chanting around the altar, they were abducted by pirates and taken to a nearby island to serve as concubines. Can you imagine?!!

I flew over Mount Olympus on the night Olympiada gave birth to Alexander. I saw an eagle fly off the summit at the exact moment the baby was born. I took it as an omen. I knew he would be great. I heard what the people were saying. They thought the baby's father was Zeus himself.

Years before, I witnessed the birth of Achilles, another great hero. Did you know that Achilles was not Greek? Does that surprise you? He grew up to become Prince of the Myrmidons. Because he was of mixed heritage, you know, his mother was the daughter of Nireus, no, not the Nireus who was the first king of the island of Symi, another Nireus, a sea god, and his father was a mortal, the gods cursed their marriage. Thetis knew that her son would die young. When he grew up, Odysseus called on him to participate in the Trojan War but because Thetis knew the outcome, she refused to let him go. She was so afraid, in fact, that she dressed him as a girl to escape the sharp eye of Odysseus who went looking for him. Odysseus could not be fooled. He saw a young girl who didn't really look like a girl and, being a shrewd Greek, he immediately became suspicious. What do you think the conniving Odysseus did? He got dressed as a merchant and walked around, calling out his wares. He was selling dolls, threads, beautiful silver and bronze stick pins, he was selling swords and hammers and welding tools. And what do you think Achilles did? He ran to check out the swords. Right then and there Odysseus grabbed him and told him to take off the feminine outfit and to be the man he was born to be.

Thetis went up to Mount Olympus. I saw her. She went to visit Hephaestus, the god of fire and metal. It seems she wanted him to make double-breasted armor for Achilles and a stronger shield so that her son should be safer in battle. And the god did comply. He did as Thetis requested. But that was not enough. That was not enough because what's meant to be is meant to be.

He was fearless in battle. Do you know what happened? Hektor, the brother of Paris, killed Patroklos, Achilles's friend. Achilles vowed revenge. He would not listen to his mother who pleaded with him, telling him that if he did so, his own death would soon follow. I saw all that as I flew over Troy, Troy the city with the fortress that kept out the enemy until that fateful night. You know, the night with the Trojan Horse. Anyway, Achilles slew Hektor. And wouldn't you know, Paris sought revenge. He aimed at the Prince of the Myrmidons. His arrow flew off the bow and hit Achilles in his heel. Do you know what I'm talking about? When he was born, his mother lit a magic fire and dipped him into it to make him immortal but he cried out. So loud, in fact, that I, too, heard his cries. I did not know just what to think. Peleus ran to see. When he saw the fire, he was furious and would not let Thetis explain. He thought that she was about to burn his child. From that point on, he would not leave the baby alone with his mother. It is unfortunate because Thetis did not have time to dip the baby's heel into the fire. And that is exactly what the arrow of Paris pierced--Achilles's heel. Do you know who slew Paris? Let me tell you. Philoktetes. That's who. He was the first warrior to be injured in the

Trojan War and had to be left behind until his injuries healed. Then he caught up with everyone. That is who slew the Prince of Troy.

Many years before that, I often flew over Minoan Crete. It was one of my favorite spots. I would look down and see Knossos. I saw the palace and the gardens, the fields, the warriors, and the Minoans. That was a civilization that is no longer. They were at their zenith around 1500 B.C. but when the volcano on Santorini erupted, they were destroyed. That's right. I have been around that long. They were quite versed in making tools as they had copper and bronze. They made the double-headed axes and they had underground and indoor plumbing. They traded. They were very smart when it came to commerce. They carried on the trade for the Egyptians who were afraid to cross the Mediterranean in their feluccas. Can you imagine such an advanced civilization afraid to cross the sea? They would look at the sea and shudder and call it "The Big Green". Unbelievable, isn't it? The Cretan men looked forbidding. The Cretan women were very beautiful, especially when they wore their jewelry. I saw the volcano erupt. It was horrendous. The soot, the pumice, all the gases were carried by the wind to Crete. The beautiful palaces were all covered in ash. The frescoes on the walls, depicting the Cretan way of life, were covered in ash. There were earthen jugs in the basements, full of corn and rice and wine. Everything was covered in ash. Some of the earthen jugs still remain today, standing where they had been three thousand five hundred years ago. I fly over the grounds sometimes. I look down and I see what used to be and what is no longer. The columns still stand. You see, the Minoan palaces had columns and so did some of the homes. Some of the walls still stand and I look at the frescoes. It was a magnificent civilization bathed in glory. When the Minoan civilization met its end, the Egyptians lost their trading partners.

Now, picture this: Athens in the year 1896. Do you know what was going on in Athens at the time? The Olympic Games, that's what. One of the contestants was a youth by the name of Spyridon Louis. He ran in the marathon and won the gold. That's right, the gold. When he was in his village, he was extremely poor. He worked in the fields picking olives. One day at a village festival, he saw a young girl dancing. Well, he fell in love head over heels and she the same with him. But guess what? She was the adopted daughter of one of the richest families in the village and no daughter of theirs was going to marry an insignificant youth. So they rejected him. He worked in the fields day and night to forget his beloved. Then he exerted his body even more. He began to run and run and run. He ran to forget. He got ideas. He wanted to run in the Olympic Games. He trained for them. I used to see him run in his village as he was training for the games. He qualified. He went to Athens to participate. I flew to Athens to watch him compete. The night before he was to run, he did not sleep. He was up all night. Any other athlete would have tried to get a good night's sleep. But not Spyridon. He stood under the stars and prayed to them all night. I saw how he prayed. Fervently. I believe in the power of light and darkness and how the two interplay for the desired effect. I believe that if you summon the power of light, it will have a positive effect. Before the games, his beloved's father promised his daughter to whomever won the gold. It reminds me of Atalanta, the beautiful, swift-footed maiden, daughter of the Arcadian King Iasos. She challenged all her suitors to a race. The youth who would outrun her would win her as his wife. The losers would be led away and put to death. Only Hippomenes had the sense to pray to Aphrodite for help and support. And she, being the goddess of love and beauty, came to his aid. Legend has it that on the island of Cyprus, the birthplace of the goddess, there grows a tree with golden leaves and branches. Golden apples grow on these branches. The goddess Aphrodite gave Hippomenes three of these apples and told him how to use them. At intervals, he threw each of these apples. And Atalanta stopped to pick them up. She stopped to pick them up and wasted time. Hippomenes outran her, won the race, and claimed her as his wife. But he forgot, or neglected, to thank the goddess for everything she did for him. And she was slighted. One day when Hippomenes and Atalanta were in the woods, Aphrodite instilled in the youth the passion for him to take his wife. And this he did in a sacred temple that had been built in honor of Rhea, wife of Cronus and mother of all gods. And Rhea punished them. Their hair became rough manes and they grew claws and tails. They growled. The goddess Rhea had turned Hippomenes and Atalanta into beasts. They had turned into lions. Just think, the daughter of the king found herself married to royalty, but not of the human race. How strange. Who would have thought? Now, let's get back to Spyridon Louis. He stood under the stars and prayed. He prayed with all his heart; he prayed with all his soul. The next day, Spyridon ran the marathon. Spyridon won the gold. He was no longer insignificant. His beloved's father had no choice. He kept his word and Spyridon Louis married the young girl of his dreams. He was a winner all around. He has made the Greeks proud. In modern-day Athens, there is a street named after him.

I fly over modern-day Athens now. Everyone is getting ready for the Olympic Games. I saw a rehearsal of the opening ceremonies. It was like a dream. A dream. A meteor descended into a pool. Flames emerged to form the five Olympic Circles, interlocked. Fire and water. The goddess Athena, holding her shield and her spear, emerged as well. The Greeks drew on their past and on their history, they drew on their present and on their mythology to create a magnificence equal to none.

They make me very proud. If you look at any of the stamped papers of the Greek Archdiocese, you will see me. Take a good look. You will see me. I am a symbol of their faith. I am a symbol of the Greek existence, I represent the East and West, the Greek ethnicity, and the Greek faith. An eagle is a proud bird and they have made me proud.

Chapter Twenty-Eight

And Greek Mythology

I really can't believe this. I have to *compete*? *I* have to compete? And with *Poseidon*, no less. Don't the citizens know who I am? Am I not important enough, *I*, the daughter of Zeus? So, I have to bribe the citizens for them to name the city-state after me, eh? Let's see....What can I do to sway them in my favor? Let me think....How many more days are left before the competition? Not too many. I really must impress the populace.

I do not like Poseidon. He is one wicked god. I know what he is capable of doing. He wants everything for himself so when he feels like it, he hits the seas with his trident and the seas become angry, covering the land, sweeping off crops, drowning the fields (much to the dismay of Demeter), and causing great destruction to the land.

Although I must give him credit for building the walls of Troy with the help of Apollo. I don't know just how they did it. They assumed the forms of men and built the walls, being promised payment in gold coins by the king, no less. Anyway, why does he have to have everything? Don't I deserve to have something, too?

I got it! I know what I will give the citizens on the day of the competition. I will offer them an olive tree. Yes, an olive tree. The olives will yield oil and this will sustain them forever. They can eat the olives and cook with the oil. Great idea! Well, what did you expect? After all, I am the daughter of Zeus, and as I emerged from his head fully-grown, holding my shield and my spear, I absorbed all the knowledge the Father of the gods had in his head.

What? What is this I hear? I will have to compete with Athena. Is this for *real?* I have to *compete? I* have to compete? And with *her,* no less. Don't the people know who I am? Am I not important enough, I, the brother of Zeus? Hey, you, plebeians, don't forget that I assumed the form of man and helped Apollo build the walls of Troy. I keep guard on the seas and do not let an enemy vessel approach. I must offer the people something that will please them. I have to win their favor. So what will the land be called? Posidonia? That sounds great! A city-state named after me. Let's see....What can I offer?

Competitions? *More* competitions? What *is* this? I'll fix her, too. How dare Arachne go around telling the plebeians that she is better at weaving than I am! Let us compete! Set up the looms! I have to produce flawless work, as usual. I cannot let her win the contest. What would it do to my reputation?

I can't believe the day of the competition has arrived. What is this I see? In her tapestry, Arachne is including scenes of the gods and their many love affairs and infidelities and their deceit with the mortal girls. *What? Their deceit with the mortal girls, too?* That cannot be! Apollo and Leucothoe? Apollo chasing Daphne? Apollo and Coronis? Apollo and Clymene? *What? Phaethon's mother?* Apollo and Hyacinth? *Apollo and Hyacinth? What?* A lad?!! Zeus and Metis? Zeus and Europa? Zeus and Alcmene? Zeus and Danae? Zeus and Leto? Zeus and Mnemosyne? Zeus and Demeter? *What? Zeus and Demeter?!!* Unbelievable! I just can't allow Hera to see that one! Oh, here is a scene of Poseidon taking Medusa in my temple. *What?* How can she possibly expose this? Do you know what that would do to my reputation? Let me take a closer look. Her work is flawless. I am very proud of her but I cannot let her know it. I must avenge this shame. I must avenge this shame the same way I did when Poseidon and Medusa lusted in my temple. I punished her. I punished her by depriving her of her most beautiful feature--her hair. *What is this now?* Arachne is trying to hang herself from a noose? I don't *think* so! I will not let her die. There!! Arachne, weave eternally!!

Why did I ever allow my son to drive my chariot? He doubted that I, Apollo the sun god, was his father. His mother told him so. Why did he doubt her? Even before I finished telling him that I would grant him any favor he asked of me, being that I truly am his father, he asked me for my chariot. I should have known better. I should have thought of the possibility that he might ask for something that would endanger his life. He wanted to control the winged horses, if only for one day. I told him it was dangerous, that he was asking for power beyond his strength, because my son was a mortal. Not even Zeus himself could drive the chariot. I told him he would have to go up a very,

very steep hill and then descend the same way. When I, myself, look down on my way to the heavens, I still get dizzy after all these years of experience. When I look up at the moving sky, I am always afraid that I will lose my balance and fall off my chariot into the swirling seas below. No, he would not listen. I told him about the fearful monsters in the sky that I have to be careful to avoid along with the bull's horns, the archer's arrows, the crab's sting, the lion's open mouth, the poisonous bite of the scorpion, and many other things that might appear before me. He would not listen. I gave him my chariot. The horses, the horses that were so used to my hold, immediately recognized the unskilled hands of the rider. They began to prance and gallop and spread their wings as they overtook the winds. Fire came out of their nostrils. Without my hold to guide them, the chariot was unballasted and careened from side to side. Phaethon did not know their names. He could not call out to them. I stood and watched in agony. I knew what was going to happen. Phaethon and my chariot would climb up very high one minute and descend very near the earth the next. I saw what was happening to the vegetation, the vegetation that Demeter worked so hard to plant and cultivate. It dried up. Actually, it was burned. My son Phaethon scorched the earth. My sister Artemis looked down from her throne on the moon and saw my horses, the chariot scorching the mountain tops, barely missing the clouds. She saw the earth catch fire and the rivers dry up. She saw the trees and leaves dry to a crisp, and cities perish and just become plain ash. Phaethon looked up. The excessive light blinded him. He could not take the heat. Dazed and stunned, he held on to the reins. His hair caught on fire. The horses bolted and the axles flew off the poles. The wheels and spokes broke into pieces. He looked down on the earth and lost his balance. I saw my son fall from my chariot. I saw my son fall into a river on the ground. And his poor mother pulled her hair and screamed out in agony but it was all to no avail. I will never forgive myself for promising my son anything he should ask for. I will never forgive myself.

I can't possibly describe to you what I felt when I saw Phaethon driving my brother's chariot. Sitting on my throne on the moon, I happened to look down one day, and what do I see? My nephew flying erratically all over the sky. I froze. Where was my brother? What had happened? What was he possibly thinking when he promised my nephew anything he wanted? Didn't he know teenagers? Wasn't he a teenager once himself? Sometimes he still can't behave himself. Anyway, I saw the earth catch on fire and the rivers dry up. I saw the mountain tops become scorched and the trees and leaves burn to a crisp. I saw cities perish and just become plain ash. Cities that had been designed and built by great architects who had come up with the ideas of domes and points. The domes were made of glass. From the moon I could see right through these domes. These buildings had musical revolving doors. I could hear the music all the way up here. The obelisk-shaped buildings were made of gold. That's right. Their walls were solid gold that sparkled, reflecting the sun's rays from their top-most angle, blinding me when my brother and his chariot flew over them. Then there were the trees. The trees that were made of glass, their crystal branches laden with fruit fashioned of pure gems. Sapphires. Amethysts. Diamonds. Rubies. The cascading waterfalls, containing gold threads, flowed into the river as it, in turn, emptied into the sea. That's right, gold threads. Where are they all now? Burned to a crisp, that's where. And why? Because my brother's spoiled son did not believe his mother when she told him that my brother was indeed his father. *Oh, no!* He didn't believe it. He wanted proof. I saw his hair catch on fire. His beautiful, long, wavy hair caught on fire. I couldn't believe my eyes! Phaethon looked down into the vast empty space between the heavens and fell into a river. It went up in smoke when he splashed into it. It burned for two whole days. My brother cried for weeks. He could not believe his boy was gone. He could not believe the destruction he saw all around him. He continues to blame himself. As for Phaethon's mother, she is beside herself with grief. She blames my brother and his stupid way of thinking. What's done is done. Nothing will bring back Phaethon. My brother has gathered his horses and the axles and the poles and all the pieces from his chariot and put them back together. He cannot stay on Mount Olympus and grieve all day and all night. He cannot neglect the earth. He has begun his route again. What can he do? He has no choice.

Oh, I really have to tell you something about these curious mortals on earth. I love to hunt. I occasionally go to the forests with my pack of hounds and I hunt deer and pheasants. I dare not touch the peacocks. They are Hera's favorite birds. You know, the second wife of Zeus. Anyway, one day I was in the forest hunting all morning and I became so weary that I decided to bathe in one of the crystal ponds nearby. I summoned the nymphs and they helped me to disrobe. Wouldn't you know it, I heard a human voice. It seems a young hunter was in the area with his hounds. He stumbled upon me as I was bathing in the pond. I was so embarrassed! I do not like to be seen nude by a passerby. I became very angry. He just stood there, in shock. Do you know what I did? I punished him. I have the power to punish anyone I want. I turned him into a deer. Yes, he became that which he had been hunting. I heard his comrades calling him. I heard them call his name. "Actaeon! Actaeon!" But guess what? He could not respond. I know he heard them and he understood because I saw the tears roll down his face but he could not respond. His hounds came upon him and he recognized them but they did not recognize him. They took him for a deer. They lunged at him. They bit and tore him all to pieces. Actaeon was ripped to shreds by his own faithful hounds. I am the goddess of the hunt. I do not like to be seen nude by a passerby.

I am also a very good daughter. I love my mother Leto and I defend her fiercely. When she was pregnant with my brother and me, our mother did not know where to go to give birth so that Hera would not find out about this relationship. You see, our father Zeus is quite unfaithful. Everybody is afraid of Hera and every place on earth rejected my mother and would not allow her to give birth there. Guess what our father did? He wished it and it happened. An island came up from the sea. He named it Delos. There my mother could give birth when her time came. To stifle her screams, the screams that go with childbirth, he created a pond in the middle of the island. My mother gave birth in the pond. One day on her way to visit my brother at Delphi, my mother was pursued by the villain Tityus. She was terrified. I saw this and I became very angry. I pursued him. You see, I have to defend my mother. Being that I am always on the hunt, I carry my bow and arrows. I reached back, took an arrow from my quiver, aligned it on my bow, and pulled the string. I did not miss my aim. Tityus dropped to the ground, dead. Not only am I a very good hunter, I am also a very good daughter.

Well, well, well. I used to be a carefree girl. Let me tell you what happened. I still remember that fateful day when I was gathering flowers with my girlfriends. I spotted a different flower, a beautiful and unusual flower at a distance, whose fragrance had spread throughout the field. I ran off by myself to pick it because I just had to have it for myself. Before I knew it, someone grabbed me from behind, threw me into a chariot, whipped the four black horses pulling it, and off we sped to an undisclosed location. I didn't recognize any of the surroundings. It was becoming dark, forbidding, and asphyxiating more and more. I fainted. When I awoke, I was sitting on a throne next to my Uncle Pluto. He told me he had made me his wife and that I would be queen. Queen? Can you imagine that? One minute I was a carefree girl gathering flowers in a field, and the next minute I was a queen. At first, I was miserable. I felt so alone. Then something strange happened. He was terribly good to me. I began to develop feelings for him and then I didn't mind having to live in a place without any sunlight. After all, he did make me a Queen. My mother came down looking for me. Hecate told her where I was and where she could find me and that she could take me back provided I had not had anything to eat in the Underworld. But that could never happen because I had six pomegranate seeds the day before. My mother was devastated. She made an agreement with Pluto. They would share me, six months each. Although I was happy to see my mother, I was also quite annoyed because that meant having to leave my beloved husband. Now she is ecstatic when I am with her but nobody considers my feelings. How do you think I feel away from my beloved Pluto? I think that mothers in general should learn to mind their own business and not meddle in the affairs of their married children!!!

I, Hera, married the philandering Zeus. I can't believe it. And if that's not all, I am his second wife. Metis, poor Metis, was swallowed by him when she was pregnant with Athena because my jealous husband was afraid that the oracle would come to pass. You see, he had been told by an oracle that his daughter would equal him in wisdom and his son would overpower him and rule the Universe. So when Metis was pregnant, he told her to transform herself into something small. She had that capability. Unsuspecting Metis transformed herself into a fly and he swallowed her. When her time to deliver was drawing near, Zeus got a tremendous headache. He summoned Hephaestus and ordered him to break his head in two. When he did, Athena emerged from Zeus's head, fully-grown, holding a shield and a spear. Then, a while later, he married me. I don't know why I married him even if he is the father of all gods. He is so unfaithful. My husband runs after so many women. And I always find out no matter how much he tries to hide his infidelities. He kidnapped Europa, a mortal girl, who gave birth to Minos. With Demeter, he fathered Persephone. With Mnemosyne, he fathered the Nine Muses. With Danae, to whom he appeared as gold coins, he fathered Perseus. With Leto, he fathered the twins Artemis and Apollo. She had to find a place to give birth because no place would receive her. Everybody was afraid of me. When will he ever learn? Did I tell you about Alcmene? With her, he fathered Hercules. I couldn't take it anymore. Do you know what I did? When Alcmene was in labor, she was calling out for the goddess-midwives to help her. I sent them along with Lucina. She sat on Alcmene's bed and watched her. You see, I had corrupted her mind. She crossed her legs and laced her hands together and spoke constricting charms. Alcmene really suffered.

She wanted to die. I was getting my revenge. Then, Galanthis, one of Alcmene's faithful servants, figured something was wrong and claimed she saw Lucina sitting there. A servant girl who claimed she saw Lucina? She tricked the goddesses. She called out that they were to congratulate her lady for having given birth. Lucina, astounded, uncrossed her legs and jumped up, freeing Alcmene to give birth. How dare she! When Galanthis broke out in laughter, the angry goddess grabbed her by the hair and twisted it, grabbed her hands and twisted them, and guess what? Galanthis changed into a little weasel. That's right. How dare she do what she did? You know, when I want to unwind and relax I go to Argos where I keep my beloved peacocks. Being the wife of Zeus is not easy. But I am his wife and I have no choice. This is the way he is and I will just have to tolerate his infidelities.

I own an entire island. It is called Ogygia. Ogygia is full of beautiful, lush greenery. The cedar trees on one end of my island spread their fragrance all throughout, especially when I light a fire and burn their twigs. Acorns, wild poplars, and cypress trees are plentiful. Hawks, owls, and other types of nocturnal birds have built their nests on the branches. Wild flowers grow in the fields. A vine, laden with grapes, winds all around my cave. Crystal clear water pours forth from each spout of the gold fountains on my island. The other day, I was weaving on my loom. I happened to look up and saw a figure descending from the sky. I recognized Hermes, the messenger of the gods. I did not know what he could possibly want. It seems he had an order from the father of all gods. He wanted me to release Odysseus, the Sailor of all sailors, and help him get back to his wife and son in Ithaca. I was devastated. You see, I was keeping Odysseus on my island because I was madly in love with him. I wanted to marry him and make him immortal but he refused. He did not want to marry me. I knew he did not love me and that his mind was on Penelope, the love of his life, but I thought I could convince him. Odysseus rejected immortality for her. Odysseus rejected me, Kalypso, for her. He was contemplating by the shore when I approached him to tell him what I had been ordered to do. He doubted my sincerity and made me swear on the river Styx that my intentions were honorable. I promised to help him. I gave him tools and instructed him as to how to build a raft.

Odysseus chopped down many trees. He sharpened each piece of wood, sanded it down, and aligned one with the other. Then he evened out the joints. I could tell he was quite adept at what he was doing. He drilled holes and hammered nails. He took extra care to make sure the plumb line was as it should be. Attaching twigs and long rods, he shaped the sides of what would become a raft, the raft that would carry him home. And in the middle of the raft, he attached an antenna and a wheel that he created from willow trees. He made absolutely sure that no water would seep in through any part of his vessel.

When Odysseus landed on shore, I was weaving a beautiful piece of white material on my loom. The other day I fetched that piece of material and gave it to him. He cut it, making sure that the measurements were accurate. Who would have thought that the material I was weaving on that day seven years ago would be used as a sail on a raft built by a man I would fall in love with and want to marry? I don't usually waste my powers granting immortality but Odysseus was an exception. I fell in love with him. He made me feel like a woman. Alone on my island all these years, I had forgotten what it was like to be with a man. Anyway, I cannot go against the will of Zeus. His word is law. He wanted Odysseus to return to his island because it was meant to be. And I complied.

I provided Odysseus with food and wine and water for his journey home. I gave him advice. I told him to consult the stars and follow them because they would lead the way. I prayed for him. Even though I was devastated, I did want him to have a safe trip back to his island, to his wife, and to his son. From what he told me, his son was an infant when he left Ithaca for Troy. It has been almost twenty years.

Now his son is a young man. I can imagine the scene in his palace when father and son meet for the first time. As for me, I pass my time weaving. As I weave, I sing. I love to sing. I try to keep busy because I want to forget. I want to forget the man who came into my life and made me feel like a woman once again.

I cannot believe what happened to me the other day. You usually read about things like this in books. The goddess Athena appeared before me and ordered me to tell my father, the King of the Phaeacians, to allow me to go to the river to wash some clothes. I am his daughter Princess Nausicaa. We have servants in my father's palace who do the wash for us. For me to go to the river and wash clothes is unheard of. I asked my father, nonetheless, for a cart on which the servants would load the dirty clothing. Without an argument he gave me what I asked for. My mother gave us a large basket full of food and a cask of wine. You see, my girlfriends were invited to come with me as well. When we got to the river, the servants unhitched the mules from the cart, allowing them to graze freely on the grass that grew around abundantly, and proceeded to wash the clothes in the crystal waters. Then they placed the clothes on the pebbles by the shore to dry in the hot noonday sun. My girlfriends and I enjoyed the delectable goodies we had brought along. One friend suggested we play ball, knowing how much I love to play the sport. She threw the ball in my direction but I did not catch it. It fell to the ground and rolled off onto the grass. I ran after it. The sight that met my eyes is difficult to describe. At first I thought I was imagining things. A man, a naked man, was sleeping under the brush. I was shocked. I felt embarrassed. I could see he was quite handsome, well-built, and middle-aged. My screams woke him up. Upon seeing what looked like a savage, my playmates scattered here and there. I felt this tremendous strength and had the courage to ask him who he was and where he had come from. He fell to his knees and offered his respects and told me he could tell I was of royal lineage. He told me that my family should indeed be proud of me and that my future husband was a very lucky man. I do not know how he knew that I was single. He told me he had been at sea for twenty days and nights, since the day he left Ogygia, the island of Kalypso. The tempestuous seas, he said, had tossed him here and there, and made it impossible for him to reach land sooner. He asked me where he was. He asked for clothes to cover his weary body. I answered him, referring to him always as "Stranger", and promised him clothes, and food, and shelter. After all, he was a guest on our island. I turned my back as he bathed in the river. I gave him clothes to wear and allowed him to ride in the cart on the way back to the palace. I also instructed him as to what to do upon reaching the palace. I told him to approach my mother first. He was to fall on his knees and ask for an audience. If he made a good impression on my mother, he would get what he wished. When we were near the city gates I told him to get off the cart and walk behind us taking care not to give the citizens the impression that he was part of our gathering. After all, I am a maiden and must watch my reputation. It does not matter that I am of royal birth.

I reached the city gates and was astounded by what I saw. The palace rose high above the thick brick walls surrounding it and from what I could see, it far surpassed the one in Troy. Its walls looked as if they were made of copper and its doors of gold. The hinges were silver; the frames crystal clear blue glass. Two dogs, one of gold the other of silver and fashioned by Hephaestus himself with his tools on Mount Olympus, stood on either side of the doors. A servant opened the palace door and bid me enter. In the hallway, thrones covered with rich velvet cloth lined the walls on either side. I assumed that the noblemen of the palace sat on them as they ate and drank. In the inner chamber there were two gold thrones for the King and Queen. I did as the maiden had instructed me to do. I approached the Queen, threw myself at her feet, and asked her to help me get back to my island and to my family. I told Queen Arete that I had been away from home for many years, that I had been tossed on the seas, and that I had no intention of inflicting harm on anybody there. I did not tell them who I was. I was not sure if I should or if I could really trust them. One of the elders reminded the King that it was not proper for me to sit on the floor. King Alkinoos rose, took me by the arm, and led me to one of the thrones, beckoning me to sit. I was clothed, fed, and made welcome. The King promised he would do everything in his power to help me. He promised to give me a ship that would surely take me home. He and the citizens prepared a banquet and organized games in my honor. During the feast, a singer sang a song. He sang of the glory of war. He sang of the feats of brave warriors.

He sang of the pain of separation and death. He sang of Ithaca and its proud king. He sang of the bravery of Odysseus in battle and of his machinations regarding the Trojan Horse. The tears rolled down my cheeks. King Alkinoos noticed this. Out of respect, he did not ask. He did not ask me who I was. I knew that deep inside, he knew. He called for the games to begin. There were athletes who were great at discus. Other men threw spears. Some were good at wrestling and some at boxing. They asked me to participate. They wanted me to prove myself. I picked up a discus, summoned all my strength, and threw it. It made a buzzing sound as it flew across the room, landing farther than the others. My audience was amazed. The King realized I was experienced in life, at sea, and at the games. He ordered his council members and his noblemen to give me a gift each. I could no longer keep silent. I revealed myself. I revealed myself and began to relate my adventures at war and those since we left the land of Troy. Their silence was resounding. King Alkinoos made good on his promise. He gave me a ship to take me home. He gave me provisions. He had his men load everything on the ship. I bid everyone there farewell. I bid Nausicaa farewell. I thanked them all. Tomorrow, after twenty years, I sail for home. I sail for home and this time something tells me that I will make it. Something tells me that I will arrive safely. This time I will finally set foot on my beloved Ithaca.

Chapter Twenty-Nine

Divine Justice

I came to America in 1920. I didn't have relatives here. I came because I had a family in Greece to support. People told me that the streets in America were paved with gold. They told me that I would make a lot of money here. I left my family in Greece, I left my village, my house, my neighbors, and the life I knew. We had a parrot in the house. He used to call my name. I used to clean his cage, the cage that my father had fashioned with his own hands. I left him behind, too. I got on the ship in Piraeus and headed for New York.

I need not tell you what those fifteen days aboard the ship were like. A bunk bed. That's what I had to sleep on, a bunk bed. But I should not really complain. Traveling in steerage, what should I have expected? However, I am not sure if the other cabins on the ship had better accommodations. I slept in a cabin that I shared with nine other men. Some of those men slept on the floor. After we all got used to our sleeping quarters, we didn't want to rotate. We continued to sleep where we had settled originally. The unsanitary conditions in our cabin were unbearable. The stench was enough to make a muscular, grown man pass out like a woman. Without a porthole, don't ask me how we managed. Nobody washed. How could we? Who gave us soap? How could we wash our clothes? Some of us wore the same clothes in bed as we did during the day. Where would we find an extra set of clothes? Most of us were dirt poor. When my fellow passengers opened their suitcases, I saw they were half-empty. Just like mine. Half-empty. What was I bringing to America? Nothing much. I came with a suitcase in which my mother put my Sunday suit, the one I wore to church every Sunday and on our high holy days. My

Sunday suit and an icon of St. Nicholas, my patron saint. "Make sure you go to church in America," my mother said to me. "Make sure you go."

On the second day of the trip, there was tremendous commotion in one of the cabins. We all ran to see what was going on. One of the male passengers was looking for his suitcase. What had happened to it? Where was it? He didn't know. He could not find it. There must have been some mix-up, we told him. He was inconsolable. He was distraught. We helped him look. I found it in storage. It was standing between two trunks, two trunks that just took up the space, two empty trunks without a cover, empty just like our suitcases and like our lives. I thought of looking down there because my grandmother's brother had worked on a ship and knew the ins and outs. He told me tales. I listened. I remembered. I brought it up to give to the passenger who had lost it. He looked at me suspiciously, grabbing it from my hands. He opened it. He opened it to check the contents of the suitcase. He wanted to make sure. What do you think I saw? I think about it and to this day I am blinded by the sight. The suitcase was full of American dollar bills. Yes, that's right, American dollar bills. I do not know how much they added up to. I do not care. How did the suitcase end up in the storage room? He had been drunk. He hid it somewhere safe, he thought, and then forgot. He did not give me a reward. He did not give me anything. He did not even thank me.

The women slept in separate cabins. Congested just like ours. I think their cabins were worse than ours because that is where the children slept as well. Children, toddlers, infants. Just as poor, just as unwashed. Everybody squeezed together in a cabin without a porthole, without any sanitary conditions. It was easy for disease to spread. We prayed a lot. We prayed that we would all be well and that we would land safely in the New World. The news spread throughout the ship like wildfire. Dysentery in the women's cabin. High fever. Vomiting. Alexena was the worst of all. Her husband was traveling with us, in my cabin. It seems before they left their village, she had just given birth. With three small children already to take care of, she had given birth to a fourth. They had been hoping for a son. Three daughters they already had. And yet, they tried again. They had been hoping for a son who would carry the family name. He would be his father's pride and joy. When she gave birth to a girl again, her husband could not believe it. "How will I marry them off when the time comes? I have no money. We barely make ends meet now. I cannot give them dowries. Wife, we will go to America. I will work and we will raise our daughters." There was no doctor on the ship. There should have been but there was not. You see, nobody cared about the poor. The poor only cared for each other.

One night we heard the news that made our blood turn cold with fear, with pity, with pain, and with uncertainty. Alexena did not survive. Alexena had died. She had wasted away because she did not have the strength to battle her illness and win. Her husband almost lost his mind. We all knew what would happen next but no one dared utter a word. We were on the high seas with another week to go before landing in New York. The order came from the captain's quarters. The body would be buried at sea. In other words, thrown overboard. What could we do? Under such conditions more disease could break out. They really had no choice. Nobody spoke. Her children were crying bitterly for their mother. They could not understand why she was sleeping so much. She would not wake up no matter how much they called out to her. Not even when her four-year-old daughter tickled her feet. That's what she used to do at home, Alexis said. She would tickle her mother's feet and Alexena would jump up and laugh until she cried. But not now. It wasn't working now. They wrapped the body in a shroud from head to toe. There must have been incidents like this aboard the ship before. They knew exactly what to do. Two sailors lifted it, tipped it over the ship's rails, and threw it overboard. They threw Alexena into the sea, to a watery grave, without having a Greek priest read the last rites, without having a Greek priest give her final communion. Just like that. Her husband went into a depression. He stood on deck in icy weather and stared at the sea. He stared at it continuously. It was the sea that had swallowed his wife, his dreams of a future together, his hopes of a better life in America.

I woke up one morning and ran up on deck to join the others. There, on the horizon, was the Statue of Liberty. She was beckoning the crowds. She was promising the poor, the downtrodden, the underprivileged like me, a better life. I had seen pictures of her in my history books in school, but I never imagined that the majesty of the Lady would be so captivating in real life.

Kastigari was an experience of its own. That's the way the Greeks pronounced Castle Garden. There we were met by authorities who were not particularly friendly to a group of poor Greek immigrants like ourselves. Families were torn apart on Ellis Island. I can still hear the wails and screams of family members who were held back and told that they could not set foot on American soil. That meant the whole family had to go back. They refused to be separated. Either the whole family stayed, or nobody stayed. Alexis was met by his uncle, his mother's brother. It seems he and all four of his children were allowed to stay. They met the health requirements.

When I set foot in New York, I did not know where to go. At the other end of the pier, I saw someone who looked like a Greek priest. I picked up my suitcase and approached him. He told me he had a room to spare but that I could only stay with him and his wife no longer than a month. But he knew somebody in Chicago who could give me a job. I took him up on his offer.

Three weeks later, I found myself in a railroad car with other Greeks who were going to Chicago to look for opportunities. Some were even going to Oregoni, they said, to their relatives and friends. They were willing to go anywhere at all for a chance at a better life. They wanted to own businesses. They wanted to be somebody special in America. They wanted to be good citizens and raise their children in the land that promised them the world. They would start by washing dishes in a "restoranti". They would work a double shift. Whatever it took. Then they would own that restoranti. And if it were a "coni restoranti", it would be worth much more being that it would only be semi-attached. A fellow passenger spoke a little English. He had managed to teach himself, he said, by listening to the rich Greek family he worked for in Athens. He had been their butler. But things became very hard for them. One day he was dismissed.

We both got off in Chicago. I did not know just what to think. It was not as bad as New York; the buildings were not as tall. It could have been my imagination but the people in Chicago seemed friendlier. The priest in New York had given me some money and an address. I had to make connections. My fellow passenger did not know where to go. I offered to take him with me to the address on the piece of paper that the priest had given me, that piece of paper that was wrinkled after being in my back pocket for five whole days and nights.

The paint on the walls of the two-room apartment the landlord showed us on the fifth floor of a tenement was chipping and I really could not tell what color they originally had been painted. I just saw greyish streaks from top to bottom. It had one window in the kitchen that looked out onto a brick wall. There was a stove at one end by the window and a white cubicle next to it. The landlord told us it was an "iceboxi". I had no idea what that was but my friend explained it to me later. That's where we could store perishable food that would be kept cool if we put blocks of ice in the cubicle. For a small fee, somebody would deliver the ice every two or three days. Then there was what the landlord called a bedroom. I saw a mattress on the floor. A greyish-white sheet covered it. I took a closer look. On the sheet I could see the outlines of human figures. How often had the sheets been changed? Who knew? I did not ask. The landlord informed us that three other Greek immigrants shared the apartment and we would all have to make do. He also informed us that they all took turns cooking a meal. If we could work things out, he was willing to let us stay. He wanted three dollars, a month's rent up-front. The priest in New York had thought of this. He had given me money for a month's rent and a little money for food. I told my friend to ask the landlord about the nearest Greek church. He looked at my friend, then at me, and he replied, "In the next town." I came to America with a suitcase in which my mother put my Sunday suit, the one I wore to church every Sunday and on our high holy days. My Sunday suit and an icon of St. Nicholas, my patron saint. "Make sure you go to church in America," my mother said to me. "Make sure you go."

The next day my friend and I, his name was Kostas, went looking for a job. I told him I was willing to wash dishes in a restaurant. I was willing to shine shoes and to clean gutters. I was willing to do anything it took to earn a living in America. Following the smell of boiling cabbage, we came upon a restaurant. There were bags full of garbage near the entrance, some overflowing, and there was more garbage strewn on the street. I saw a sign on the top, near the roof, with writing and I assumed that it was the name of the restaurant. There was another sign on the door. The lettering was bold and black. I read the first word and understood it. "NO". This word was Greek. And it meant the same in my language. No what? The second word I did not understand. But I understood the third word, "NO". That was still followed by another word I did not understand. I walked up to the door and reached for the handle. Kostas grabbed my arm. "No," he said. "Don't bother." He dragged me away. I was furious. I wanted to ask for a job. I needed the money. Kostas looked at me. He explained something to me that shot like an arrow through my heart. It made my brain burn. He told me I had turned red, red as a beat, and for a few minutes, he was afraid I would burst an artery. Kostas explained to me in Greek that the sign on the door of the restaurant read: "NO DOGS NO GREEKS".

I ran back, grabbed the handle, opened the door and flew in. I took the customers by surprise. A heavy-set man, his shirt sleeves rolled up to his elbows, came up to me. I could smell the alcohol on his breath. His reddish complexion gave his habit away even more. I looked at the stained apron wrapped around his bulging stomach. The stains were deep-set. It hadn't been washed in weeks. Kostas, on my heels, was pulling me towards the door, screaming "*Ela, ela,* come on, come on." I didn't even have time to open my mouth. The burly man came up to me, grabbed my arm, and pushed me. "Get out of here, you stinking Greek." That's what he said. "You stinking Greek". I cannot tell you what I felt when Kostas explained it to me. I could not understand why the Greeks were so unwelcome in some places in

America. Where were the Greek communities? Where was the Greek section in Chicago? Where were the opportunities?

Kostas asked around. He went here and he went there. Holstead Street. "That's where we will go. That is where the Greeks live. That is where they work." We went. We couldn't believe our eyes. There were Greek restaurants, Greek grocery stores, Greek coffee shops. I was transported to Greece without even getting on a ship.

I got a job in one of the Greek restaurants. I washed dishes on a double shift. I made what I thought was a lot of money. I sent money to my mother in the village. She sent me her blessings. I made more money. I rented a room, by myself, in a boarding house in the area. I could not believe my good luck. My employer liked me a lot because I was a hard worker, quick, careful, and never missed a day. And I never broke a dish. I saved my money. I had my plans.

My boss had relatives. They had daughters. It was time, he said, for me to find a nice Greek girl, get married, and start a family. But the daughters of his relatives were in Greece. "I will show you some pictures. You will choose the one you like."

Six months later, at thirty-five, I was a married man. My boss and I made the five-day trip to New York. I married my wife on the pier the minute she got off the ship. Right next to her trunk. The minute she stepped off the ship she had to get married; otherwise, she could not stay. Those were the laws. The priest whom I had approached when I first set foot in New York years ago, married us. The bride got married in her gray cotton dress with the ruffled hem and the high collar and long sleeves. But she was beautiful. Her smile melted my heart, the heart that she had won when I first saw her picture. My boss was our koumbaro. Then we all traveled back to Chicago to go on with our lives. A year later, I was a father. My boss and Kostas baptized my son. We baptized my son in the Greek church "in the next town" for good luck. By then, Kostas had gotten a job, too. He made the best demi-tasse this side of Greece in Mr. Yiorgos's coffee shop.

The years went by. I bought the restaurant. That's right. I bought the restaurant where I began washing dishes twenty years before. Now I hired somebody else to wash the dishes for me. I hired a waitress to serve the customers Greek food. Patsa-tripe. Arni-lamb. Pasticcio. Mousaka. Lentil soup. Soupa avgolemono. Magiritsa on Holy Saturday night and Easter Sunday. Retsina. Mavrodaphne--the dark, sweet, red wine the Greeks love so much.

My boy grew up. He wanted to take over the family business but I did not want him to do that. I wanted him to go to the University. We argued. I won. He went to the University where he studied business. Then, he came back here and managed the restaurant. It was time for me to cut down on my work. I had worked too hard all my life. I let my boy take over. I could see he worked zealously. He loved what he was doing. And he was good to me. He wanted to send me and my wife on a trip to the old country. He wanted his parents to visit the land of their birth, especially after so many years. I had not been back to my village since I left for America in search of a better life. My wife was eighteen years old when she left her village to come to America to marry me. My son wanted us to take this trip, fully paid by him, as a token of his appreciation for everything we had given him when he was growing up. I would not hear of it. "Only if I bring back a nice Greek girl for you," I joked.

One day my son came home and announced that he had something very important to tell us. His mother and I could not imagine what it could be. He was in love, he said, and he was getting married. Just like that. He was in love. *Whom* was he in love with? Where did he meet this woman? Did we know her? *And,* was she Greek? The second generation of Greeks, American-born, of course, and around my son's age, was beginning to emerge in the community.

It pains me when I think of it. He brought her home to meet us. She sat at our table for dinner. She did not finish the food on her plate. "It tastes strange", she told my son. I looked at her. I kept looking at her, at her red hair, her freckled face, and at that wry smile. I could not seem to remember where I had seen her once or twice before. She did not even look at my wife all night. For her, my wife did not exist.

They got married. I do not know in which church. We did not go. No son of mine was going to marry a girl who was not Greek. No son of mine would disgrace the family like that. My son's children would not be Greek. Half-Greek to me is not good enough. I wanted to disown my son. My wife became distraught. "If we disown him, what will we have? He is our only boy, our only hope." I did not say a word.

The restaurant was doing well. He asked me if I would go there for a few hours a day to help him with the customers. My son knew how to speak Greek; that was not a problem. He wanted me to help him collect the money his customers would give him. And they gave him money. Plenty of it. I went. I went because it gave me something to do and because it was my link between

America and my culture. I spoke Greek with the customers. And they spoke Greek with me.

One day, I looked across at the shops around my son's restaurant. It seemed that they were still the same, still the way they were on that first day when I set foot in the restaurant and started washing dishes. I looked across the street and I saw her. I saw her talking to a man. I do not even want to call her by her name. For me and for my wife, our son's wife does not have a name. She does not have a name, she does not have a face, she does not have a place in our lives. But she has a place in our son's heart. Or so it seems. Who was that man? He seemed quite old, or older. I could not tell. I could not tell because it seems life did him in. But his facial features reminded me of somebody I knew. Or thought I knew. He was a thin, bent man, with a reddish complexion that gave away his habit. His shirt sleeves were rolled up to his elbows and his stained apron was wrapped around his stomach. The stains were deep-set. It hadn't been washed in weeks. My son read my mind. "He is my father-in-law," he said. It all sank in. A shiver went up and down my body. My heart began to beat quite fast and I began to sweat. "Your father-in-law?!!!" My son looked at me with trepidation in his eyes. I did not say another word. I looked at my son, I looked at her, and I looked at her father. Her father, who years before, had the nerve, yes, had the nerve to call me a "stinking Greek". And yes, his daughter had married my son. The son of that "stinking Greek".

My little grandson calls me "pappou". He melts my heart. I talk to him in Greek. And when I do, his mother leaves the room. She does not like it when I speak my mother tongue. She cannot understand our ways. Only a Greek woman can understand a Greek. My little grandson has my name. He tells me that when he grows up he will marry his yiayia. I tell him he cannot do that because his yiayia is already married to me. He tells me he wants to have a wedding in New York by the pier. Just like his pappou. I tell him when he grows up I will take him to the village and I will find him a nice Greek girl just like his yiayia. His eyes light up. My little grandson looks like me. I know that he is Greek. The other day he picked up the cover from the garbage can in the back of the house. It was his shield, he said. His shield like the ones the ancient Greek warriors used to carry. Like Alexander the Great. To me, my little grandson is great. When he grows up I will take him to my village and I will find him a nice Greek girl to marry. Just like his yiayia.

Chapter Thirty

America, The Beautiful

I am a picture bride. It was arranged that I come to America to marry the man who had sent my godfather his picture. He sent his picture and expected me to do the same with him. I did.

The year was 1922. We were not safe in Smyrna. My parents worried that something terrible would befall the family. They wanted to get me out of there as soon as possible, just in case. It was therefore decided that I accept the marriage proposal of this complete stranger, of this man I did not know, because it meant security and freedom. I know my mother was upset. She did not speak for days. But what could she do? She packed my trunk. In it she put embroidered sheets that had my initials skillfully woven on each corner, with the pillow cases to match. She added two silken robes and nightgowns, a silver tray, bronze candlesticks, a woven quilt that my godmother had made for me, and satin slippers that my father had picked up the last time he was in Tsesme, a Turkish city on the shores of the Aegean Sea.

My father was a jeweler. My mother always wore a gold cross around her neck, a cross that was embossed with filigree and encrusted with emeralds. My father had given it to her on the day he went to her parents to ask for her hand in marriage. The night before I was to leave for America, my mother gave me two rings, heirlooms that belonged to my paternal grandmother. She also gave me some advice. I was to hide these rings so that the Turkish sentinels in Galata, the area where the ships docked, would not get wind of them. She was sure they would search my trunk. I was to keep these rings safe in America.

The *Megas Alexandros* was a huge passenger ship, or so it seemed to me. It was impressive like the Macedonian warrior after whom it was named. I could not believe that I, the daughter of a rich jeweler with so much money for his daughter's dowry, was forced to make the trip to a world I did not know. A fate like this was usually expected of a girl who did not have anything to her name.

Very early the following morning, my parents and two brothers escorted me to Constantinople, to Galata, where I would board the ship. I wanted to see the Turkish *mahalades*, the Turkish neighborhoods, one more time. I knew that it would be the last. Father was adamant. I dared not disobey him. I took the two rings Mother had given me, my grandmother's two rings, and put them in my mouth. Yes, in my mouth. I attached each one on a tooth on each side of my lower gum, near the back. Mother gave me advice: "Be good to your husband. After all, he is the reason you will be staying in America, the land of opportunities. In time, you will learn to love him." I thought of the picture I had seen. I had seen a tall, handsome man in a three-piece suit, a folded coat over his arm as he stood in front of a barber's shop. It was a barber's shop, my godfather said, because there was a red and white pole in front of the shop's window by the sidewalk. Red and white? The picture was a black and white. My godfather told us that the young man in the picture was a furrier. He made a lot of money. Mother told me that in due time, I would be very happy.

I remember standing on the pier waiting my turn to board. The next few minutes are more or less a blur. The Turkish sentinel called out to me. He asked me what I was carrying in my trunk. I told him everything I knew. His partner grabbed one of the Greeks. He grabbed one of the Greeks for no apparent reason and pushed him to the ground. He raised his club and hit him over the head. I saw the blood trickle from the side of his head. I screamed out. I screamed out so much that one of the rings that had been attached on my tooth fell out. I froze. The sentinel who had asked me what I was carrying in my trunk approached me. He smacked my face. He smacked my face so hard that the other ring fell out as well. The two rings, my grandmother's heirlooms, were taken by the Turks. What could I do? Nobody, none of us, said a word. Mother just held me in her arms. She could not stop crying, all the while saying that she did not know when she would see me again, *if* she would ever see me again. Father, however, appeared to be quite stoic. He did not say a word. All he did, and I remember distinctly, was hug me once and pat me on the head the way he did when I was a child. When I was his beautiful, vibrant, energetic child, the daughter of a jeweler, the daughter of a jeweler who could have had the world on a silver platter.

It took two weeks to reach New York. But I did not get seasick. I was used to the sea; I loved the sea. I had learned to swim at the age of three and I was like a fish in the water, Father often said. I often took a walk around the deck to exercise, to reminisce, to breathe the fresh salt-sea air, and to unwind. I was trying desperately to sort out my life. I did not know this man, this man who had sent my godfather his picture. And I was terribly afraid. But he did not know me as well. How could I live with a complete stranger? Would I ever feel comfortable with him? Would I ever get to love him? I did not know. I only knew I had no other choice.

When the ship docked, there was so much commotion. I disembarked and stood on the pier, my trunk by my side, my eyes searching for the handsome man I had seen in the picture that I kept in my pocketbook on my arm. I saw someone approaching me. With him was a Greek priest all decked out in his church attire, holding what seemed to be a Bible. I looked at the man coming nearer, a smile on his face. I did not recognize him even though he did call out my name. He introduced himself to me. He introduced himself to me and if I could, I would have boarded the *Megas Alexandros* for the return trip to my home, to the world I knew before, and to my family. This man was tall all right, and I could see a slight resemblance to the man in the picture but there was something else. He was not that handsome stranger I had seen. What happened to his wavy hair? What happened to that hair that resembled the waves of the Aegean Sea? This man was bald. And he looked so much older. I tried to figure out his age. It seemed to me that he was even older than my father. And when he smiled, I saw the gold. No, not the gold rings that I had so foolishly lost or given up, but the gold tooth on the right side of his mouth, the gold tooth that added years to his appearance and made him look so old.

The priest married us right then and there. What could I do? In order for me to stay in America, I had to have a wedding by the pier. A church wedding was out, being that I needed to be somebody's wife immediately to even walk on the streets of New York. As a child, it was always my dream to wear my mother's soft silk wedding dress that I had seen in her wedding pictures. The silk gown that flowed down her beautiful statuesque body as she stood next to my father on the day their lives became one. I had always dreamt of putting on her veil, the veil that covered her beautiful face, the face with the ivory skin and Grecian features. In her wedding photos, my mother is holding a bouquet of lemon blossoms. Lemon blossoms for good luck and for the marriage to last a long, long time. And here I was. I was standing next to a stranger, a complete stranger, in my everyday dress that I had worn on the ship as I strolled around the deck, dreaming of America and of the life I left behind. The service was over before I even knew it. The priest had brought along a set of "stefana", or wedding crowns, and it seemed to me that he used the same ones for every couple he married by the pier. And who was our "koumbaro"? Who was this man who served as our best man? The priest's friend. The priest's friend who served as a koumbaro at every wedding the priest conducted by the pier of New York. I thought of Ellis Island and the scrutiny. Perhaps it would have been better had I been barred from entering. I would go back. Go back to what? I did not know; I did not think.

I did not have a wedding photo to send to my parents back home. I would not have a wedding photo to remind me of the day my life changed, that day when the carefree girl I used to know became somebody's wife. I would have nothing to show my children and my grandchildren. I did not say a word.

I always dreamt of my hometown and those I left behind. Sometimes the dream was so real that I could feel my mother near me and I could even smell her fragrance. There, there, I stretched my arm and I could touch her cheek. I could smell my father's pipe and hear the logs crackling in our fireplace. Then I would wake up and find that it was all a dream. I would wake up and realize that I was far away from home in a strange room, in a strange house, and in a country I could not learn to call my own.

We had been married a few months. A letter came addressed to me but it did not come from my beloved Smyrna. I noticed right away that the stamp was not Turkish, but Greek. But I recognized my mother's handwriting on the envelope. I did not know what to make of it. I opened it with trembling hands. To this day, and many years have gone by, I still remember what I was wearing on that day, I remember what my husband had told me that morning, I remember what I had been thinking before I got my mother's letter in that envelope.

She wrote from Mytilene. In that letter she wrote me all the news, all the events that had taken place since I boarded the *Megas Alexandros* in Galata and headed for America. One morning, they heard gun shots. Yes, gun shots. Everybody ran out to see what that was all about. That's how the Turks got all the Greeks to come out of their homes. And then they shot as many of them as they could in cold blood and killed them. Just like that. No reason. Just like that. Or maybe the Turks did have a reason that made no sense to the Greeks. The Greeks were businessmen. They were teachers. They were accountants. The Greeks were doctors, lawyers, priests. They were law-abiding citizens who minded their own business. They were very successful in a land that turned out to be something else other than their home; something else other than hospitable no matter what it seemed like in the very beginning. The Greeks, in reality, were foreigners on foreign soil. Or, should I say, foreigners on enemy soil? I could not finish reading the letter. I wanted to die right then and there. I wanted to go back to my Smyrna, to my home, to my old life. I wanted to turn back the clock. I couldn't. I took a deep breath and continued to read. There was panic and confusion. There was screaming, yelling, crying and death, maiming and mutilation. My mother wrote that they were ordered to leave. What about all the wealth we had in the house? Leave it behind just like that? She would not hear of it. The Turks gave her no choice. They ran. On their way to the pier, to the boats waiting to take them to salvation, she saw my godfather, my godfather who had shown me the picture of my husband. He promised me a good life in America. My mother saw him by the central water fountain where we gathered on summer nights to talk and to cool off. He was holding his hands under the spouts. What hands? The stumps that were left after the Turks cut off both my godfather's hands because he was a merchant. This way, he could not unfold the yards of material anymore to show his customers. That was his punishment. My Uncle John had lost his mind. He was my father's brother. He lost his mind when his two beautiful daughters were raped right before his eyes by a group of Turks.

I did not finish reading her letter. I folded it, put it back in the envelope, and slipped it in my apron pocket. I did not want to know the rest. I asked not of my father and two brothers. Maybe she wrote about them, too. I do not know. I do not want to know. I wrote her back. It took a long time for me to answer my mother's letter. In my letter I asked her, no, I pleaded with her not to mention my father's fate and that of my brothers to me, ever. I wanted to be in the dark. I wanted to be ignorant. I wanted to remember them the way I used to know them when I was back in Smyrna and we were one big, happy family. I was about to mail my letter to her new address. I held it in my hands and looked at it. I held it in my hands and kissed it. I kissed my mother, my father, my brothers, my uncle, his family, my godfather, his family, my home, my Smyrna, and my old life. I kissed Smyrna's beloved soil that I had known as home. My husband stood there watching me. I did not care if he thought I was crazy. Then I saw him put his hand in his back pocket. He came up to me and put a fifty-dollar bill on my lap. "For your mother," he said to me. "Put it in the envelope and send it to your mother."

I looked up at my husband. I did not recognize him. I saw a tall, handsome man in a three-piece suit standing in front of me, a folded coat over his arm, his wavy hair blowing in the wind. I saw his smile and I noticed how straight and white his upper teeth really were. "Be good to your husband," I heard my mother say. "After all, he is the reason you will be staying in America, the land of opportunities. In time, you will learn to love him."

I have been married twenty years. I cannot understand one thing. My husband has not aged with time. I want to know his secret. I tease him about that and he just laughs. Twenty years and my husband is still that handsome man with wavy hair. Sometimes I see him in my dreams. He is standing next to a red and white pole in front of a barber's shop. Then I wake up. I wake up and next to me in bed, I see my husband, that handsome man with wavy hair, the man who is the reason I have stayed in America, the land of opportunities.

Chapter Thirty-One

A Greek Sailor's Log

I was born in Denmark in December of 1410. My mother was Greek; my father was Danish. He had been a naval officer and met my mother in Northern Greece where his ship had docked for repairs. She was tall, dark, with almond-shaped brown eyes and a warm, beautiful smile that could melt the polar ice caps. He was tall and dashing. His blue eyes met hers on the steps of the church where she had gone to light the votive candles. My father was on leave and had decided to take a stroll around the square, eventually ending up by the town church. My mother spoke no Danish; my father spoke no Greek. Yet, they were able to communicate with one look, just one look. It was enough for him to ask for her hand in marriage. My grandfather did not know just what to say or what to think. Part of him was upset because his one and only daughter was not marrying a Greek; part of him was very happy because his one and only daughter was marrying a man who was respected, had a government position, and could promise his wife a good life. Above all, he was also very handsome. My grandfather gave his consent. The wedding, the Greek wedding, took place two weeks later in the church on whose steps my parents had first seen each other. Of course, the whole town was invited to the wedding. The whole town and the entire crew of my father's ship.

My mother traveled with my father the first few months after they had been married. Whether or not she was happy traveling on the high seas with him, I do not know. But that did not last very long. It did not last very long because my mother wanted to give birth to me somewhere on the shore, somewhere on land that I could claim as my legal place of birth. I was born in Copenhagen, Denmark.

December, 1428

I have been hired to work on the *Copenhagen*, a ship that has been commissioned to sail around the world for educational purposes. I am very fortunate that I was accepted, being that the sea is in my blood and I cannot live far from it, on shore, doing just any kind of job. As a matter of fact, I could not even force myself to enter the University. Father was devastated. But I am eighteen years old and I feel that I am entitled to do what I truly think I should. I cannot wait to sail on the high seas, to experience adventure, to explore the world, to learn from my experiences. I believe that this will be an education that cannot compare to any I would have gotten at the University.

Second week of December, 1428

In a few hours we will be docking in Montevideo. We had a good trip, relatively speaking. We did not hit high seas and that was good because I was able to walk around on the deck. I admired the five tall masts, the masts that absorbed the wind when it blew, allowing the vessel to sail its course without mishap. I would smell the salt-sea air, and just think and unwind. I often think of my home and of Denmark. Mother was worried sick when I told her what I had been planning to do. She wasn't happy with my decision because she had experienced life on the high seas. And to make things worse, she had had a bad dream the night before I sailed.

Middle of December, 1428

We are now sailing for Australia. From Montevideo, I mailed my parents a letter informing them of my safe journey. The voyage to Australia will take several weeks, the captain informed us. We will sail around the tip of South America, and find ourselves in the Pacific Ocean. I have heard tales of Papua, New Guinea. I have heard that Papua is the home of the world's most horrific cannibals. The tribes fight among themselves. They fight for the captives. The victim's heart serves as a meal for the leader of the tribe. This way, it is believed that the leader will increase his strength. I have heard tales....

The Captain informed us that he has sent a message back to Denmark: "Voyage on schedule and going well."

I often stroll on the deck. This morning I noticed what looked like land on the horizon. The Captain told me it is an island. He mentioned the name but I cannot remember it well. I think he said it is called Tristan Kouna.

That's strange. Our Captain informed us this morning that the Danish Coast Guard is sending out ships to look for ours. That's strange because they just received his message that everything is going well. Why would they want to do that?

April, 1929

We are now sailing for Australia. The voyage to Australia will take several weeks, the Captain informed us. We will sail around the tip of South America, and find ourselves in the Pacific Ocean. I often stroll on the deck. This morning I noticed what looked like land on the horizon. The Captain told me it is an island. He mentioned the name but I cannot remember it well. I think he said it is called Tristan Kouna. The Captain and I continued to stand on the deck and both of us saw a ship a short distance away. It seemed as if it were following us, always at the same distance away. It could not catch up to us; we could not distance ourselves from it. We looked more closely. It was a battleship. Why was it coming after us? Oh, wait. It was a fishing vessel. Of course it could not catch up to us. Our ship was much too advanced. But wait, it was a battleship. That's what it was. A battleship.

That's strange. Our Captain informed us this morning that the Danish Coast Guard is sending out ships to look for ours. That's strange because they just received his message that everything is going well. Why would they want to do that?

Our Captain just received a message of distress from Denmark. He read it to us out loud: "ATTENTION ALL VESSELS: The *Copenhagen* is now considered lost at sea."

The Copenhagen? The Copenhagen? That was our ship. Surely, there was some mistake. Some terrible mistake. Here we were. Here we are sailing on the high seas, on our way to Australia. This was indeed a serious mistake. Perhaps the Admiralcy intended to write the name of another ship. That's it. The name of another ship.

July, 1930

What is this here before us? I cannot make it out that clearly because of the dense fog. It looks like a commercial ship. Our Captain sent a message. The Captain of that other ship informed him that we were sailing very near Peru. We are sailing for Australia. The voyage to Australia will take several weeks, the Captain informed us. We have sailed around the tip of South America, and find ourselves in the Pacific Ocean. From here, it shouldn't take that long.

September, 1930

I often stroll on the deck. I noticed something on the horizon. I saw strange sculptures on the land, being that we were so close. Some of them were shaped like columns. The Captain and the other men aboard saw the same thing. But we did not see life. We only saw the sculptures. One of the sailors told us he had heard about this island in the Atlantic Ocean. *The Atlantic Ocean?* Yesterday we had been sailing in the *Pacific Ocean* on our way to Australia.

November, 1931

I often stroll on the deck. This morning I noticed what looked like land on the horizon. The Captain told me it is an island. He mentioned the name but I cannot remember it well. I think he said it is called Tristan Kouna.

February, 1935

I often stroll on the deck. This morning, I noticed something on the horizon that frightened me. I saw what looked like glaciers. The icebergs were so tall; they looked as if their peaks were scraping the sky. I am almost certain that they must be 500 feet above the surface of the sea. They were drifting at what seemed to be 0.4mph. I know. I looked at the instruments. That's strange. Icebergs are prevalent in the Arctic and Antarctic regions. How can that be? We are sailing for Australia. There were sheets of ice floating in the water. We will sail around the tip of South America, the Captain informed us. From Montevideo we will go to Australia. There are small pieces of ice floating in the water. What is this I see before me? It looks like a bottle. There are humongous icebergs all around. There is no way out. We are surrounded by them. What is this bottle in the water? I can see more clearly now that it has come so close to the side of the ship. There is a note inside. It is in my handwriting. That is my handwriting. Let me see what I wrote..........

50.0N/45.5W 420-370 South -020-14'
Latitude and Longitude
HELP! We are surrounded by humongous glaciers with no way out.
SOS. We are sinking!

Chapter Thirty-Two

A Dream Fulfilled

There is a Greek saying: "Vouno me vouno then smiyee". Only a mountain does not bump into another mountain.

When you tempt Fate, you get what you deserve. Having gotten a Master's Degree in English Literature with a concentration in Elizabethan English, don't ask me what came over me for me to take the Modern Greek Exam the Board of Education gave a few years after my college graduation.

Fast Forward.

Picture this: a classroom full of fifty-one Greek teenagers That's right. I was teaching a singleton class full of native Greek students. A singleton, a class that was one of a kind on its level with no other class of its sort in the entire school "Pedia!" "Class!" I tried to get their attention above the din. Did I say din? Make that party time. When Greeks get together, it is party time indeed. Oh, and another thing. There is nothing you can teach a Greek student being that he already knows everything, everything from the minute he is born. If you are a female teacher, that is a strike against you. If you are an American-born teacher, that is a strike against you. If you are an American-born female teacher, that is two strikes against you.

BUZZ!! What was that? Oh, the bell. Time for change of class. Oh, now I have to switch gears. I have to teach in English. This constant zig-zagging and switching gears is making me awfully dizzy. I am getting seasick. You see, I am not a Greek sailor and I cannot take to the sea all that well.

BUZZ!! Oh, the bell. Think Greek. Teach Greek. BUZZ!! Oh, the bell. Think English. Teach English.

This went on for ten years. I educated my students; they educated me. We had our good times; we had our bad times. They contributed to building Athens Square Park, in my opinion, the most beautiful park in the whole wide world. Located in Astoria, it is a legacy to Hellenism. The park features a monumental area where three Doric columns are the focal point. There is an amphitheater around which cultural affairs are orchestrated. Athena, the goddess of wisdom, greets visitors at the main gate and Socrates transports the visitors to the Athens of two-thousand-five-hundred years ago. It was originally planned that the statues be sculpted in marble. However, due to the unfavorable weather elements of New York and the possibility of vandalism, they are sculpted in bronze instead. The statue of Socrates is composed of seven-hundred pounds of solid copper and bronze. Yes, seven-hundred pounds of solid copper and bronze. The statue of Athena, a gift from the city of Athens, is also a blend of copper and bronze. My students sold tee-shirts. Tee-shirts with a picture of the park as a decal. They collected ads for the committee journals that were distributed at the annual dances. And they were proud. They were proud because they, too, contributed to the gift that the Greeks and Greek-Americans built as a token of appreciation for everything that America has given the Greek immigrants.

Picture this: an English classroom full of freshmen who think they are still in Junior High School We must read <u>The Good Earth</u>.

They do not seem to be interested no matter how hard I try to introduce it in a variety of ways. I think of a strategy. We will write a play based on the novel and we will act it out. We will change some parts. I will bring props. We will have a lot of fun. Only one class is interested. It seems that this class was sent from serendipity to act out <u>The Good Earth</u>. In the entire class, there is only one female student. One female student who would make the most perfect O-lan. She plays her part. She plays her part so perfectly. So perfectly, in fact, that one would think she was truly O-lan in another life; O-lan from the paper page come-to-life in this life, come to life in front of an audience. And Farmer Ming. We made him up. He carried a coolie across his shoulders and distributed red eggs to his neighbors and to the audience members for good luck. Then there were the guards. There was Wang-Lung. Wang-Lung, O-lan's husband. The student who portrayed Wang Lung had been failing. He had done nothing much all term long. He played Wang-Lung. He played Wang-Lung with such conviction, we heard the Chinese accent in his speech.

Perfectly. A born Wang-Lung. He brought the audience to tears. He passed the class. He passed the class because with his performance, he showed us how much he had learned. He showed us how much he had learned from books, from school, from life.

When I was a little girl, I used to play school with my dolls. They were my students; I was their teacher. It was my dream. It was my dream to become a teacher. I wanted to reach out. I wanted to make a difference. I wanted to educate.

Picture this: one week before my college graduation It cannot be! But yes, it was. Helen. Who? You remember, Terry's mom Helen, the Garment District, the subway on my way to school....My mom and she crossed paths. After all those years, their paths crossed on the street. She asked my mom about me. And my mom filled her in. Her Fay was getting her degree. Her college degree in teaching. It was a dream-come-true. It was a dream-come-true because America is the land where dreams can become reality, where dreams can be fulfilled.

Chapter Thirty-Three

Holiday Anecdotes

I never knew my grandparents. My maternal grandmother was still alive when I was born but I never got to meet her. My yiayia was not educated and she could not read or write. She lived on the island with my aunt. I used to send her my pictures. I used to send her letters. I didn't yet know how to write but I sent her letters, nonetheless. I would sit on my mother's lap and she would hold my hand. Together, we traced letters. We traced the letters that made up the Greek alphabet. And I wrote to my yiayia.

One Christmas season when I was four years old, my mother wanted to send them something special. We couldn't send them money or anything expensive, but it was the thought that counted.

There was a Woolworth's in my neighborhood. A booth stood in one corner. One could enter that booth and cut a record. All for a quarter. That's right. A quarter. I knew some Greek Christmas carols that my Mother had taught me. As a child, singing came naturally to me. For my grandmother, I sang all the Christmas carols I knew. I even asked her how she was doing. When my recording time was up, we waited a few minutes, and lo and behold, a record slid out through the slit in the machine. We sent the record to my grandmother. They didn't have a phonograph but one of their neighbors did. They played it on her RCA victrola and heard it through the cone after winding the handle attached to the piece. Half the island heard my record. I brought great pleasure to my grandmother. You cannot put a price on pleasure of this sort. You cannot put a price on a gift of this sort. It certainly was worth more than the twenty-five cents it cost to cut the record.

Every year around the Christmas holiday, the afternoon Greek school I attended as a child was abuzz. We were all getting ready for the Christmas pageant. On that night, some of us would recite poems while others participated in duo presentations or even entire dramatic scripts. However, for us children, the most important part of the evening was the time when somebody's father, dressed as Santa Claus, would come out of somewhere, or out of thin air and proceed to give out little gifts from the sack on his back to all the students in the auditorium.

One year, in contrast to my life, I played the part of a rich little girl. I was holding a beautiful doll that had been a gift from St. Nicholas the Christmas before. My partner, not as affluent as I, asked me to give him her address in hopes that she would get a doll just like mine. I promised her I would. But I forgot. I forgot to give Santa Claus her address and I did not worry about it. On Christmas morning, she woke up to find a beautiful doll just like mine waiting for her. That puzzled me. It puzzled me because I could not figure out how he knew where she lived.

Chapter Thirty-Four

A Greek is a Greek is a Greek

Greeks are simply wonderful when it comes to hospitality and philanthropy. No one can dispute that. They have a very big heart, big enough to fit the whole wide world. There is a Greek word in our vocabulary that is difficult to translate. It is "filotimo". Only a Greek can understand. Filotimo is when somebody's yiayia is sitting at the table next to yours and all she is having is coffee. You offer to treat her to pastry or spanakopita or tiropita and do not take any money when she offers to pay for what she cannot afford. Filotimo is when you buy Greek foodstuffs for a friend who lives in another state where there is not one Greek store to be found. You send the foodstuffs to your friend and do not take his money. Filotimo is when you remember what your friend, or your neighbor, or your aunt or uncle did for you to help you out some twenty years ago. Or thirty years ago. Filotimo is when you are embarrassed to look your father in the eye after you do something wrong. Filotimo is a feeling that rises from deep within your soul, from your Greek soul, and chokes you, and tells you how to feel. It tells you how to think and how to act. When it comes to filotimo, the Greeks win the gold medal.

Try to change a Greek and see if you can. I don't think so. If you ask a Greek for the time, he will look at you and ask if you are going somewhere, or have to be somewhere, that time is so important to you. You see, a Greek does not care if the sun rises, if the sun sets, or if it doesn't set at all. To a Greek, time does not mean a thing and life is one big party.

He may not care about time, but there are some things that he is passionate about. What are these things? Let me tell you. He is passionate about life. He knows how to enjoy it and he will tell you that he is just like Zorba the Greek. A Greek knows how to dance. He knows how to dance to that bouzouki music like no one else on earth. When a Greek dances, he is transported to a different plateau. His friends watching him dance are equally passionate. So passionate, in fact, that they throw plates on the floor of the club and break them. They throw flowers at the singers up on stage. Then they pay for everything. They pay for everything because they are passionate with filotimo. A Greek is passionate about his mother. And about his sisters. *His* mother, not yours, not mine, not anybody else's, *his* mother is the best mother on Earth. Don't argue with him about that for you will never win. As a matter of fact, you will never win any argument with a Greek because he is always right, whether he is right or not. So when he tells you that his mother is the best mother on Earth, shake your head yes and agree with him. Because, if you don't, he will remember. And if he sees you standing on a street in Athens looking for a cab, he will not pick you up even if his cab is empty and even if he happens to be going to wherever you want him to take you. It's bad enough he will not change course and take you wherever you want to go if he *does* like you, let alone if he *doesn't*. You will remain standing on the Greek sidewalk until another cab comes by with three or four or five other passengers inside. Then you will have to sit in the trunk. You will have to sit in the trunk because a Greek cab driver will pick up as many passengers as he can and take them not to where *they* want to go, but wherever *he* wants to go. A Greek is passionate about his cigarettes. He does not care that he pollutes the air. Don't bother to write a law prohibiting smoking in public. He will smoke no matter what, no matter where. And while he smokes, he will drink his Turkish coffee and absorb it all. Don't even think of calling it Turkish coffee in front of a Greek. You can call it Greek, you can call it demi-tasse, but you can't call it Turkish. You see, a Greek forgets that the heavy duty coffee with the thick coffee grinds originated in the Middle East and was introduced to the Greeks by the Turks when Greece was under their subjugation for four hundred years. Don't argue with a Greek because you will never win. He will make up stories to convince you that you are wrong and give you reasons why the coffee should be called Greek instead of something else. A Greek is passionate about his worry beads. He is absolutely passionate about them and he takes them everywhere. It is a ritual. He clicks continuously no matter where he is and what is going on around him.

So now, picture this: a Greek in a Greek coffee shop smoking his cigarette that contains tar and nicotine above the normal, puffing smoke and polluting the air, sipping his demi-tasse, clicking his worry beads, and reading his Greek newspaper Any questions?

Don't bother to ask any Greek a question. Questions confuse a Greek. He is so confused himself, he will give you a round-about answer and be so good at it, that after a while you will see things his way, you will believe everything he tells you, and you will consider him a genius indeed.

So now, picture this: my first trip to Greece, my mother and I in a cab in Athens, a cab driver who wanted to impress his two passengers by telling them about the geography of the United States He was so good, indeed, that I told him he ought to be commended on his knowledge because he knew U.S. geography the way no American knows U.S. geography. So, for those of you who did not know, let me tell you that Brooklyn is in New Jersey, Philadelphia is in New York, and Connecticut is in Boston. So there!

Greeks are very hospitable. Ever since the time of the Olympian gods, the Greeks have been hospitable to friends and strangers alike. Thus, in keeping with the traditions of our ancestors, we offer number one hospitality to anyone who visits.

By the way, you better be home when a Greek comes to visit. It doesn't matter that he didn't notify you ahead of time and you were not expecting him. You just better be home anyway. A Greek will tell you, "Oh, one of these days I will stop by." He will leave it at that. Then, if he stops by two years later, he expects you to be home. If you are not, he will be highly insulted and will think that you left your house on purpose so as to avoid his visiting you. You better have a good response when he tells you that he told you he would be stopping by. So, make sure that you stay home and wait for the Greek to visit you whenever he pleases, day or night, rain or shine.

A Greek house is always obvious. It is obvious in the entire neighborhood, stands out, and sets off the alarms. You can't miss it. You can't miss it because the garage door is painted sky blue and white. Why sky blue and white? Let me tell you. It is painted sky blue and white because those are the colors of the Greek flag. His front door awning is sky blue and white. He has the Greek flag hanging from the post in front of his house, or he has the Greek flag hanging from his bedroom window, or he has the Greek flag hanging from some-where. He has the Greek flag hanging from somewhere because he wants you to know he is a Greek and that he is proud of it. Some of them even go as far as putting up a sign in the front, right on the living- room window: ELLHN

That clinches it. He is telling the whole wide world that he is GREEK. And then there is the lawn. He wants to be absolutely certain that you know he is a Greek so he erects Greek statues on his lawn, right in front of his house. The statues depict the Greek gods. Or they depict Greek historians. Or they depict Greek warriors. Maybe even Greek statesmen. Among the most popular ones are Zeus, the father of all gods, Apollo, the god of the sun and of music, Thucydides, the historian, Pericles, *the* ancient Greek statesman, and Alexander the Great with his head tilted towards the East. Sometimes, and that is rare, he will put up a statue of Athena, the goddess of wisdom. Notice that almost all the statues on a Greek lawn are male. Why is that, you think? You don't know? They depict males because a Greek is a chauvinist. He loves women, he adores women, but he is a chauvinist. He cannot tell a woman that he loves her. The fact that he has married her is enough. That alone should suffice.

And when he marries her, he stays married for forever. That's right, for forever. When a Greek wears the wedding crowns on his head on his wedding day, he honors them. He honors them by making the marriage work. He honors them by making himself lord and master of his house, he honors them by making his presence known in his house, and he honors them by telling everybody in his house what to do, what to think, and what to say. And that includes the wife, the children, the in-laws, the siblings, the nieces, the nephews, the neighbors, and the friends. He is free to go anywhere he wants, to do anything he wants, to think anything he wants, and to say anything he wants. As a matter of fact, he tells everybody that his wife is married but he is single.

A Greek knows how to live the good life. To him, it is always party time.

And the wife helps to make him feel like a king. A Greek woman treats her husband like royalty. A Greek wife takes excellent care of her husband. He stands by the sink but will not get himself a glass of water. Instead, he calls out to his wife to come from wherever she may be to get him the glass of water and practically put it in his hands. She will help him put on his coat, his bathrobe, and his slippers. She will put his slippers on his feet for him just like Cinderella and the Prince. Or, should I say, just like Cinderello and his servant-in-waiting. When he gets sick, his wife will call to make the appointment with the doctor. If he doesn't want to go for a check-up, she will practically drag him to the doctor's office and then, after the tests, she will call the doctor and consult with him over the phone in regard to her husband. When he gets a cold, she will make him a cup of tea for his sore throat, she will rub his back with alcohol, and she will feed him chicken soup. A Greek woman waits on her husband hand and foot. A Greek woman worships her husband.

A Greek is very proud. He is proud of his heritage, his religion, his village, his island, his language, his flag, his national anthem, his family, and his children. But most of all, he is proud of his family name. A Greek is so proud of his family name that there is a saying in Greek that, roughly translated, says that it is better to lose an eye than it is to lose your good name. And his daughters better live up to this reputation, otherwise, there will be pandemonium in the house. Or, he better not find out.

A Greek is fanatic about his religion. He will build a church eveywhere and anywhere he migrates, he will give money to the church, he will go to church, and he will teach his children to do the same. If he should marry out of his faith, which is very rare indeed, he expects the wife to assimilate, to practice the Greek religion, to raise the children in the Greek faith, and to learn to speak the Greek language. He expects his wife to learn to speak Greek, to cook Greek food, and to become Greek. Period. No questions asked. He, of course, is not obligated to reciprocate.

A Greek has a big pocket. He will give to the poor, he will give to the rich, he will give to the widows, he will give to the orphans, to the downtrodden, to the underprivileged and to the misbegotten. And when a Greek gives you his word, he keeps it.

A Greek remembers. When you do him a favor, he will remember for forever. And he will reciprocate. And he will be grateful. He will be grateful to you, to your family, and he will also be grateful to the second country that he has learned to call home.

Chapter Thirty-Five

Reflections

I, Fay, who am like firecrackers but not like putty, born under the sign of Virgo, fear dogs, elevators, and aging, like flowers, babies, and computers, dislike grapes, sarcasm, and failure, love teaching, dancing, and justice, am a GIFT to this world because I move mountains.

Five things I cannot live without:

1) family and friends
2) my books and my writings
3) my computer
4) my condominium
5) chocolate

Five things you will find in my bedroom:

1) my computer
2) a bridge to my heritage via my icons, especially my three-dimensional replica of the Monastery of Panormitis sculpted on a plate
3) my beautiful clothing
4) my bed
5) my memories of my past enveloped in pain

Two things I am absolutely passionate about:

1) Greek mythology
2) ancient Greek

My favorite place to visit:

the island of Symi in the Dodecanese, in Greece

My favorite colors:

red and black

Red is one of my favorite colors. It is one of my favorite colors because it reminds me of me. It is a bright color, full of life and energy. Just like me. It is also passionate. Just like me. Black is also one of my favorite colors. It is one of my favorite colors because it is somber and sexy. It is a sad and serious color. Just like the other side of me.

My favorite flower:

Red carnations are my favorite flowers. The red color reminds me of my bright and full-of-life personality and the multi-folds of the carnation resemble my intricate and complex self.

Chapter Thirty-Six

A Mosaic

I'm not too comfortable up here on the roof. The adults, my mother included, are perched on the two-foot wall that serves as a barrier between the roof and Kingdom come. My mother seems very comfortable with heights. A persistent odor, as if something has gone stale, keeps permeating my nostrils. It is the tarred roof.

The adults are laughing and talking. They are all immigrants. Some are from Italy, some from Hungary, the Ukraine, and Poland. My mother is from Greece. There are other Greeks on the roof. They are all able to communicate with each other without a problem even though some speak more English than others. They understand each other. You see, they share the same pain. Occasionally as they are talking, they throw a glance towards the direction of the Hudson River that leads to the Atlantic that leads to Europe that leads to their beloved countries, their villages, their islands, and their towns. Ah, the horizon....The vast horizon that leads to their youth and to the love and security that surrounded them many years ago. But poverty does many things. It is like wine. It brings man to the brink of despair. Not thinking clearly, he makes life-altering decisions that stay with him forever.

Whenever I bump into Signora Lina in the hallway, she calls me "bella ragazza". A student I may be, but I certainly don't consider myself beautiful. However, it's very sweet of her to say it. I have tremendous respect for her. She, too, has a cross to bear. Her husband, a window washer, accidentally plunged to his death when their only child was four years old. She did a great job raising her son. Fast forward: When I was graduated from high school, Signora Lina gave me a card accompanied by a bottle of cologne. The raised designs arranged in rows all around the glass bottle resemble bricks. The bottle is shaped like a tower. Years later, the bottle with the cologne still inside, stands on my dresser. It ties me to my past and reminds me of Signora Lina's pride in my accomplishment.

The Hungarian woman on the second floor is a widow, too. She has a beautiful daughter who resembles Rapunzel. The daughter has long, golden hair that she wears braided around her head. That's strange! I get confused. My maternal grandmother on the Greek island wears her hair the same way. How is it possible for people to resemble each other like that? The young girl is very talented. Every time she sings opera, we hear her up on the fourth floor. It is through her I get my first taste of classical music. For a woman left a widow many years before, the mother struggles to provide her daughter with every amenity. Sometimes it is not opera we hear. The daughter screams at her mother. They speak in their native tongue and we do not understand what they are arguing about. It doesn't matter. We all bump into each other in the hallway and exchange greetings. One day, we learn of the mother's sudden death. I am terrified. An inexplicable fear grips my soul. I want to jump out of my skin but I can't. It is as if I am trapped in a tower. The bricks are tightly cemented together. The mortar is unbreakable. I am suffocating.... Her sixteen-year-old daughter, lucky she, however, was rescued by a prince who was blonde, handsome, and Hungarian. That same prince we saw kissing her on the lips as the two of them sat on the lower steps of the staircase on the ground floor. I can't breathe....

Mrs. Ellen, the super, is from the Ukraine. She is a widow. Like Signora Lina, she, too, lost her husband when he plunged to his death as he was washing somebody's windows. Her grown son lives with her. Her apartment is the warmest in the entire building. You see, Mrs. Ellen has a pot-bellied stove that she keeps burning all day long. That is where she cooks the Ukrainian sausage whose delectable scent travels through her quaint kitchen to the hallway, permeating all four floors. She is a great super. She keeps out the drunks, the derelicts, the drifters, and everybody who does not belong in the edifice she loves so much. We all feel very safe there. She is also the only one who has a phone. Whenever my mother and I need to make a phone call, we go to her. She does not understand our tongue. We keep it short and, at the end, we put a dime on her dresser by the phone. Sometimes she takes it; sometimes she does not. It depends on her moods. To my mother and to me, a dime is a lot of money. It goes a long way. Fast forward: One day, we hear that she is ill. The doctor makes a house call. A few days later, the doctor makes another house call. We do not know what is going on. But we all think about her and we are concerned. Then, she is transported to the hospital. A short while after that, Mrs. Ellen dies. Her building is not the same; our building is not the same.

Mrs. Callas on the floor below ours is a gem. Her full Greek name is Kalogeropoulos but her husband Americanized it for business reasons. You see, in order to acquire some things, you must give up others. Mrs. Callas is a widow and lives with her brother in order to make ends meet. Sometimes, on hot summer days, her brother Tom buys us a pint of ice cream from the drug store in the Port Authority. Mrs. Callas, my mother, and I share it and consider it a treat. All for twenty-five cents. Mrs. Callas is very educated. When she was in Greece, she was studying to be a teacher. She instills in me a fierce love, a passion for Greek mythology. Mrs. Callas baby sits me when my mother has to go shopping. She never takes money from my mother. Sometimes I behave myself; sometimes I don't. When she baby sits, she reads to me. She reads tales of gods and goddesses and of the heroes and demi-gods of ancient Greece. She transports me to Mount Olympus. She reads me fairy tales in English and then translates them into Greek. She has probably read me "Cinderella" a thousand times. "The Three Little Pigs" is a must. "Sleeping Beauty" follows. What happened to the grandmother in "Little Red Riding Hood"? Since when does a grandmother get such treatment? Why must the wolf swallow the grandmother who ties you to your past and to your culture? Why are some fairy tales so gross and cruel? I love Mrs. Callas very much. She considers me the grandchild she never had and she considers my mother the daughter missing from her life. The other day, I decided to celebrate my doll's birthday and throw a birthday party. I invited Mrs. Callas. She came to the party and brought my doll a box of vanilla marshmallow cookies.

Thea Yiannoula on our floor lives directly above Mrs. Callas. She was married when I was born but her husband was sickly and he died when I was a child. He owned his own business. He was a shoemaker. Thea Yiannoula does not know how to read or write because when she was growing up in her part of Greece, they did not believe in educating the girls. Either Mrs. Callas or I write her letters for her. Thea Yiannoula has a heart of gold. When a neighbor gets sick, it is Thea Yiannoula who appears at his door with a tray of food. Thea Yiannoula heard my father fall when he suffered a fatal heart attack. He was in the hallway and she was in her bedroom. It was Thea Yiannoula who ran to him first to offer what assistance she could. When she reminisces about her life in Greece, she shows me the dance she used to do as a girl, the dance that is the most popular in Sparta. It is the "tsamiko" and it is the national dance of Greece. The friendship between Mrs. Callas and Thea Yiannoula goes back many years. Maybe forty years. That is how long they have been friends. When one needs the other for assistance, they communicate by banging on the radiator pipes. They have devised this system as neither one of them has a telephone.

I have come home from school to find that Mrs. Callas has been taken to a Greek nursing home as she is no longer capable of taking care of herself. My heart is broken. Our house is forlorn and empty. I cry but things do not change. I miss her. I miss my grandmother.

A few months have gone by. I have come home from school to find that Thea Yiannoula has gone to the same nursing home to be with her life-long friend. I cry. I miss Thea Yiannoula. I try to ease the pain by looking at pictures. I have pictures of Thea Yiannoula as she is standing on the roof, the clock tower and the Hotel Manhattan in the background. Her hair is braided and it is tied around her head and held in place by a small hair net. That's strange! I get confused. My maternal grandmother on the Greek island wore her hair the same way. How is it possible for two people to resemble each other like that? In the picture, I am a few months old and Thea Yiannoula is holding me. In the picture, I am a few months old and Thea Yiannoula is holding me in her arms. She is holding me in her arms the way a grandmother holds her grandchild.

My mother works in a factory. During her lunch hour, she comes home and washes the clothes. Then she hangs them on the clothesline on the roof to dry. They blow in the wind. My father, a baker on a ship, is on his way to Piraeus. He will sail back in a few weeks. Then he will be on his way to Piraeus and back to New York over and over again. They are awaiting my birth. By the time my mother comes home from the factory, the clothes are dry. She is tired but she is of strong character. She grabs the helm like a Captain whose ship is about to be sunk by inhumane, angry, uncontrollable gale winds. She steers the ship into calm, balmy waters. She has faith in herself. She believes in this country. This is America. The sun always rises.

About the Author

Fay N. Kozas is presently an English teacher in a New York City public high school and has also taught Greek literature in the past. She earned a Bachelor of Arts degree from Hunter College and a Master of Arts degree in English Literature from St. John's University. She recently published a book on Greek/Jewish haiku and has had several literary works, including Greek poems, published in various American and Greek newspapers. She was instrumental in the construction of Athens Square Park, a recreation area that serves as a symbol of the legacy to Hellenism. This is the author's first publication of anecdotal literature.